Doug —
Saw this @ book sale!
Library Bathroom reading ???

Fly The Airplane

Meredith Tcherniavsky Holladay
and Dana Holladay

Mom

(Seems like it contains
some aviation wisdom?)

ISBN: 0-6157-3649-1
ISBN-13: 9780615736495

Dedication

To Alex.

Preface

by Meredith Tcherniavsky Holladay

I began writing this book in January 2009, during what I can only hope will turn out, at the end of my days, to be the most emotionally wrenching and physically exhausting period of my life.

It started as a private diary of the pain I was experiencing as my first marriage unraveled, a way for me to organize my thoughts and feelings so they might begin to make sense. As I continued to write during that difficult year, I realized something larger was taking shape, something that had the potential to change my life forever. I dreamed of quitting my job and leaving my old life behind to launch on a quest of self discovery, which to me, as a pilot, meant exploring America in a small airplane. I pursued several funding options and even wrote a business plan for the trip, but just couldn't figure out how to find the time, the money and the courage to actually pull it off.

I thought maybe my trip would be the basis of a book. Maybe my planned adventure, and the story I'd write about it, would transform my suffering into something positive. Maybe I could show the world that human beings can survive anything if they really want to, that there is happiness, peace and love on the other side of every dark cloud. But I'd have to navigate through my own storm, and prove that theory to myself, before I could show anyone else the way.

It wasn't until I met a fellow pilot and kindred spirit named Dana Holladay in March 2010 that my writing started to gel into something tangible and meaningful. You couldn't have offered me a million dollars to believe that in a little over a year after my first marriage fell apart I'd be in a healthy new relationship, writing the story of how three little words gave me the strength to move forward.

The funny thing is, they weren't the three little words I always thought would save me.

Fly the airplane.

The most important lesson a pilot learns during flight training is to never give up control of the airplane, no matter what happens. If a gust of wind blows you sideways during a landing, add full power and go around for another try. If the engine stops running, keep flying the airplane while you look for a safe place to land. Use every available resource to find a solution to the problem, and ask for help if you need it.

This book is the story of how the lessons Dana and I learned as pilots helped us to stay focused during the tough times in our lives before we met, and how a common passion for aviation brought us together in the aftermath, across many years and many miles. It concludes with the story of our journey across America in the summer of 2012, in a restored 1938 Piper J-3 Cub—the trip that evolved from the one I had envisioned taking by myself, in an attempt to find my center.

The majority of the book is written in my voice, with the exception of Chapter 4, which is written from Dana's perspective. We each contributed to the content, and Dana provided substantial technical editing throughout. All names used are those of real people, though some names have been omitted or abbreviated out of respect for the individual's privacy.

Some of our friends and family members said we were crazy when we told them we'd bought an airplane and were going to take two months off from work to fly it around the country, carrying little more than toothbrushes, a few changes of clothes and a camera. We simply smiled, thanked them politely for their concern and turned our attention to our goal: to live a life that's larger than anything we'd ever known before.

Each day is an opportunity to do something incredible. We want to show you that you don't have to be wealthy to enjoy a rich and rewarding life. You just have to get out there and make the best of what you have right now.

We're not suggesting everyone who reads this book should become a pilot, though of course we're always eager to support aviation enthusiasts. Instead, we hope *Fly The Airplane* will inspire you to seek your inner strength and follow your own path to happiness. Listen to your heart. Live each day to the fullest. Never give up on yourself. You can do it.

Fly your little airplane, and remember that if you don't like the direction you're headed, you can always change course. You are the pilot in command of your life.

"Get busy living, or get busy dying."
Tim Robbins as Andy Dufresne in *The Shawshank Redemption* (1994)

Acknowledgements

Our flight across America in the summer of 2012 and the subsequent production of this book would not have been possible without the love and support of so many people. But there are a few individuals and organizations who deserve special thanks:

- The dozens of family members, friends, acquaintances and total strangers who donated money toward our trip expenses in exchange for a signed copy of this book.
- The individuals and families who opened their homes and hangars to us during our trip.
- Fellow pilot and adventurer Patrick Moon, who lent us his SPOT Satellite Messenger, the emergency features of which, fortunately, we never needed.
- The Aircraft Owners and Pilots Association (AOPA) in Frederick, Maryland, and the Experimental Aircraft Association (EAA) in Oshkosh, Wisconsin, who helped spread the word about our project.
- McHenry Savings Bank, of McHenry, Illinois, for financing our plane.
- Mark and Ty Neal, Andrew Kim and Perry Smith, for hiring Dana, which allowed him to relocate to the Washington, D.C. area.
- All of our family members and friends who supported us through good times and bad.
- Jeb Burnside for his review, edits and suggestions on the manuscript.

Chapter 1
Survival is a Choice

Pilots are supposed to be strong, smart and responsible, with above average decision-making skills. Like doctors, police officers and fire fighters, we're trained to stay cool and focused under pressure. We use checklists, follow established procedures and act methodically to guide our machines through the sky. Still, despite our best intentions, plans can change suddenly. Life can surprise us. We can surprise ourselves.

The regulations that govern the actions of all pilots in the United States impart grave responsibility for the lives we carry onboard. Rule number one: "The pilot in command of an aircraft is directly responsible for, and is the final authority as to, the operation of that aircraft."

That means that no matter what happens, the pilot has to keep flying the airplane. We can't click on the hazard lights and take shelter under the next highway overpass when it starts raining so hard that we can't see through the windshield. We can't leisurely roll onto the shoulder and call a tow truck when we break down. We have to keep it together. We have to keep flying.

There is an incredible sense of liberation and satisfaction that comes with the responsibility of acting as pilot in command of an airplane. Flying forces you to live in the moment, to continually evaluate your circumstance and decide whether to continue on your present course, or change direction. It challenges you to make rational decisions based on data and actual performance, not emotional decisions based on fear and wishful thinking.

2

Taking off is optional, but landing is mandatory. Land or crash. Those are the only two possible outcomes of any flight. Even if you fly with a parachute attached to your body or to your airplane—which most of us don't—you still have to make the decision to deploy it before it's too late. Survival is not guaranteed. It is a conscious choice that each of us has to make every day.

Fly the airplane. Those words echoed in my head as I prepared for my first solo flight in the spring of 2002. It was late in the afternoon on a Wednesday, and the sky was painted with brilliant streaks of red and purple as the sun began its slow descent toward the horizon. After a few takeoffs and landings with me in the tiny, two-seat airplane, my flight instructor got out, handed me the keys and asked if I was ready to try a few on my own.

Flying solo is a rite of passage for student pilots, much like getting a learner's permit to drive a car is for teenagers. It's also a prerequisite to earning a full-fledged pilot certificate. I was just five years old in 1977, when my father earned his private pilot certificate. I remember lounging in my pajamas in the back of our woodgrain-paneled Chrysler station wagon on Saturday mornings, watching my dad practice takeoffs and landings at the Westchester County Airport in New York. I thought of him on that day, 25 years later, when it was my turn to take to the sky alone and prove I had the right stuff to become a pilot.

When a flight instructor clears a student to fly solo, it means the student has demonstrated the ability to act as pilot in command of the airplane under limited, carefully supervised circumstances. Usually a first solo takes place at the student's home airport, in good weather with little wind. As the student gains more experience and confidence, the instructor will allow the student to venture out to other airports, in stronger wind. But there are no safety nets, tethers or training wheels to save the novice student pilot from her mistakes. She is up there alone, and has to be prepared to handle whatever happens during that first short flight.

On the afternoon of my first solo at the Montgomery County Airpark near Washington, D.C., the air was calm and, to my surprise, so was I. As I started the engine and prepared for my first takeoff in that red and white Cessna 152, I felt a rush of confidence and happiness that I'd never felt before. At that moment, in that little airplane, it was as if all at once my mind and body came together in perfect harmony. I was in my happy place doing what I was meant to do. It was just me and the airplane, working together as a perfectly synchronized team. I knew then that the real me had arrived, that the person I wanted to be was ready to show her face to the world.

I was becoming a pilot, but slowly. I trained and studied for eight months before I had built up enough self-confidence to fly on my own. Stalls were my biggest challenge. Before a student pilot is allowed to fly solo, she has to demonstrate recovery from an aerodynamic stall. A stall occurs when the continuous flow of air over the wings is interrupted, usually as a result of the pilot getting too slow during the final approach to the runway. Unless the pilot corrects by lowering the nose and adding power to get air flowing over the wings so the airplane can keep flying, the airplane will lose more lift, sink deeper into the stall and descend rapidly toward the ground.

What should have been comforting to me as an anxious pre-solo student pilot is the fact that stalls generally don't happen suddenly or without warning. Rather, a stall is usually the result of a chain of events committed by, you guessed it, the pilot in command. In other words, the airplane won't stall unless I make it stall—either intentionally, such as to demonstrate a stall and recovery from a safe altitude during a flight exam; or unintentionally, by not paying attention to my primary responsibility of flying the airplane.

As the wings begin to lose lift in advance of a stall, most airplanes will give the pilot numerous physical and audible cues that something is amiss. Students are taught to recognize these cues and take action to prevent a stall from occurring. The yoke or stick will feel mushy in your hand instead of firm, sort of like how a car's steering becomes less responsive when driving on a slippery surface like ice or snow. Many airplanes are equipped with a mechanical device on the leading edge of one or both wings that senses the pre-stall airflow disturbance, and activates a buzzer or horn in the cockpit to alert the pilot to take action.

The antidote is simple enough on paper: Fly the airplane out of the stall. *Don't just sit there and let it happen; do something about it.* But in flying, as in relationships, it's not always so straightforward. If the stall catches the unwary pilot by surprise, she might not react quickly enough, or worse, in her panic and confusion, she might do the wrong thing and turn an otherwise non-event into a violent spinning dive. Unfortunately, most inadvertent stalls occur at low altitude, where the pilot has little time to respond, and little room to recover.

It took me years to recognize that the knowledge and skill required to keep an airplane out of trouble in flight could be applied to my life on the ground. I had to learn to be pilot in command of my own mind, body and destiny, not just pilot in command of my airplane. I had to learn the hard way that the only person whose actions and happiness I could control, was me.

***

Relationships are a lot like airplanes because they require regular maintenance to perform at their best. The two partners in any long-term relationship are like a flight crew. When two pilots fly together they have to communicate effectively with one another, share responsibilities, and always be on the lookout for signs of trouble. Sometimes, though, problems develop insidiously and are difficult to detect. Unless you make the effort to identify and troubleshoot problems as soon as they are discovered, you might find yourself dealing with a real emergency.

Wasn't the oil pressure a bit higher when we took off an hour ago? I don't know. Maybe it's the same. It's within the normal range, so maybe I shouldn't worry about it. Did the alternator warning light just flash or was that the sunlight reflecting off of my beautiful diamond engagement ring? Does the engine sound like it's running a little rough to you, or is there something wrong with my headset? Everything else seems fine. What do you want for dinner?

Pilots spend many hours training to deal with emergency situations, but humans are generally unprepared for the failure of a relationship. We don't walk down the aisle expecting our marriage will end before death does us part. Instead, we stare optimistically at the blue sky above us, strap in, fire up the engine and take off, often without really doing a thorough preflight inspection of our relationship, and of ourselves.

By the time I passed the exam to become a private pilot on February 6, 2003, I already knew something was broken under the hood of my marriage. I just didn't know what it was or what, if anything, to do about it. Flying offered me an escape from the stress I felt in my life on the ground. In the airplane, things made sense. I relied on the laws of physics and aerodynamics to provide the order and predictability I so desperately craved in my personal life. I often recalled a line from one of my favorite songs by Sheryl Crow: "If it makes you happy, then why the hell are you so sad?"

Each partner in a marriage must communicate with the other to effectively manage the relationship. Assumptions about what the other partner is doing, thinking or feeling can lead to disaster. The same is true among pilots. In the cockpit we use a procedure called *positive exchange of flight controls* to manage workload during a flight. Most airplanes have dual controls so the pilot (usually in the left seat) and the copilot or instructor (usually in the right seat) each have equal access to the primary controls needed to fly the airplane. However, only one person can act as pilot in command at any given moment. If I'm in the right seat and it's my turn to fly, the pilot in the left seat will say, "You have the flight controls" and let go. I'll reply by saying, "I have the flight controls" as I take over. Accidents have occurred when, for whatever reason, neither pilot was at the controls of the airplane because each thought the other was flying.

During that period of increasing uncertainty at home, I focused my energy on flying and earning the advanced ratings I needed to become a flight instructor. I began teaching in the summer of 2005 and had a full student load immediately, thanks in large part to personal recommendations from several of my mentors and fellow flying club members. During my first year of teaching, I earned about 70 percent of what I made at my previous full-time office job, which I thought was pretty good for a self-employed flight instructor. I began to realize I could get by on my own doing what I truly loved, if I had to someday.

While my confidence as an aviation professional continued to blossom, my personal life wilted from neglect. When I was in the airplane I felt there was no problem I couldn't handle. But at home, there was no checklist or manual I could consult to try to figure out what was wrong or how to fix it. I felt sad, tired, guilty, frustrated and angry, the gamut of emotions people experience when faced with the end of a long-term relationship.

By the fall of 2008, I knew divorce was imminent and there was nothing more either of us could do to save our marriage. I confided in close friends and family for emotional support, but the weight of it all was too much to bear. Then one day the marriage imploded, and there was nothing left to do except stumble away from the wreckage and start my life over again.

After we separated in early 2009, I spent most of my time at the airport, trading tales of adventure in the sky with the guys in my flying club. They were, and still are, like the big brothers I never had as an only child. They made me laugh and provided a sense of safety and security when I felt scared and alone. When I was around other pilots I felt respected and appreciated, but maintaining my confidence and composure in the wake of the emotional fallout of my failed marriage was a daily struggle.

Toward the end of that year, I had an opportunity to fly a full-motion, twin-engine airplane simulator at a work conference in Daytona Beach, Florida. During one of my takeoffs the instructor failed the left engine almost immediately after I'd left the ground. Many twin-engine airplanes are extremely difficult to fly on one engine, because the operating engine creates a strong yawing force to the opposite side. As I struggled to keep the plane in the air with the dead left engine hanging on the left wing like a giant paperweight, my instructor shouted, "Don't ever give it up! Fly that airplane until there's dirt in your mouth, but don't ever give it up willingly!"

The simulation was so realistic, and his directive so urgent, that I was actually sweating. My knees hurt from pressing the right rudder pedal to the floor with my full body weight just to keep the virtual plane flying straight. It was a physical challenge, just as it would be in a real airplane, but with my instructor's advice and encouragement I was able to "land" the simulated airplane safely. I thought, maybe I can survive my real-life engine failure too. Maybe if I just have a little faith in myself, I can look down into the abyss as I soar above it, and get on with my life.

Chapter 2

Restarting a Dead Engine

On Friday, February 5, 2010, "Snowmageddon" began to grip the Washington, D.C. area. I was working in downtown Washington that day and most offices, including mine, let out early due to the approaching storm. About six months earlier, I'd taken a full-time office job with benefits to boost my financial bottom line in anticipation of the divorce, while I continued instructing part-time on the weekends. Not wanting to go directly home from the office, I decided to see a movie. It was snowing lightly when I walked to the theater from the subway station, but had become more intense by the time I trudged home in the encroaching darkness. My legs were numb from the cold, wet wind and my head heavy with the knowledge that I'd be spending the next few days holed up alone in the house, with only my dog for comfort and companionship. I loved that dog more than anything, and though I truly felt he listened to me, what I really needed was someone to respond, somebody to hold.

So that night, on the advice of a good friend and fellow pilot, I poured a glass of wine, pulled my credit card out of my wallet and signed up for an account on Match.com, a singles Web site. Writing my profile felt like an exercise in fantasy fiction, because at the time the person I described was not the shattered woman slouched on the sofa, but the strong woman she knew

lived inside her, the woman who flies airplanes. I presented myself as the person I wanted others to see, with the hope that I
could actually be that person again, if only someone would give
me a chance.

I posted a photo of me taken the previous summer as I
landed on a grass strip in upstate Pennsylvania with a student
and his girlfriend. It was the only photo I had of myself in which
I thought I looked happy.

*Writing this profile was a little scary for me. Maybe it
scared you, too. But I'm the kind of person who looks fear in the
eye and works hard to embrace change, rise above the pain of
being human and find the good and the light and the beauty in
new, uncertain situations, like dating.*

*I guess you could say I'm a passionate student of life. I
enjoy reading books, traveling and seeing new places, but not in
a touristy way. I like to venture off the trail and see things for
myself, at my own pace, as they really are.*

*Music, to me, is poetry in three dimensions—the rhythm
and meaning of the spoken words, the physical pleasures of hearing and feeling the sounds, and the lesson that a good storyteller
can impart. I carry my iPod everywhere and find that listening
to my ever-expanding music collection is an integral part of my
daily life. I would really appreciate a special friend who felt
a similar connection to music, who would want to share that
with me. I do not play an instrument but I've been told I have a
decent singing voice, which I enjoy exercising in the car, with the
moon roof open and the windows down on a warm, sunny day.*

*I enjoy taking photos and would enjoy wandering
through the world with someone who also likes to observe his
surroundings with a curious eye. I have a 9-year-old four-
legged mutt who is the love of my life and always will be. We
enjoy going on long walks or jogs and hikes together, but not*

so much in the winter. Neither of us is a huge fan of the cold weather or winter sports. I basically hibernate through the winter, but thrive in the warmer months. I can't see myself spending the rest of my life in the Washington area for this reason—a quaint house on the beach or on a warm country lake is more my speed. I need to live near a body of water. I don't like wearing shoes or wool coats, and get a kick out of driving my stick-shift car barefooted.

I am what most would call a "Type A" person and tend to work quite a bit to advance my career, but not at the expense of family and friends. I go to bed early, and love waking up to see the sun rise.

Why am I here on Match? I'm not entirely sure. I guess I've reached that point in my life where I've decided it's time to open up a bit, meet new people, and maybe have a little more fun. I'm in no hurry to dive into a long-term relationship, but do hope to fall in love again someday, with the right person. For now, I'd be happy sharing a home-cooked meal on a lazy Friday night, a bottle of wine and some good music, a jog through the park, or a flight—yes, I'm a pilot—with a warm, gentle soul who knows how to make me laugh.

It didn't take me much more than an hour to write that profile, which I posted the next morning after waking to find my doorstep covered in a two-foot-deep pile of blowing snow. I never imagined I'd find myself pushing 40 and searching for love in the dark on the Internet. I wondered if passion and romance were real, if men even knew what those words meant. I'd been in a series of long-term relationships more or less continuously from the time I met my high school sweetheart at 17. Two decades later, I didn't have much to show for my efforts.

It was time to forget about all the mistakes I'd made and focus on getting in sync with myself. So I pulled out my best-looking jeans and shirts, visited a fancy salon for a fresh haircut and color, and decided to get back out into the world and have some fun just being me. From January through mid-March of 2010 I exchanged emails and phone calls with six men I met on Match.com, resulting in 10 dates. They were all very pleasant and provided a good diversion from sitting alone in the house with the dog, but I didn't connect with any of them in a meaningful way. I was a bit disappointed in how my first foray into dating was going, but kept telling myself this was just part of the process of reinventing myself as a single woman. It was a social experiment of sorts, and if it didn't work out, something else eventually would stick.

Then, on the afternoon of Friday, March 26, 2010, I received an email from a 48-year-old, divorced father of a college-aged daughter, who identified himself as a flight instructor. In his profile he wrote:

> I grew up in Richmond, Virginia and recently moved to the D.C. area after living in Chicago for 22 years. I don't believe in a perfect match, but chemistry, mutual interests, honesty, respect, and a little flexibility will get you pretty close. Every relationship has roadblocks, but it's how we navigate the roadblocks that speaks volumes about who we are and where the relationship is headed. I am not at all demanding, but I will not compromise when it comes to honesty, trust, and respect. I value my integrity and I live my life by The Golden Rule.
>
> I am compassionate, sensitive, loyal, fun-loving, upbeat, and usually quite comical. I can laugh at myself when I screw up and I always ask for directions if I am lost. I respect everyone's position, even if I don't agree with it. Life is short, so I play hard! I am looking for someone who is easy-going, independent, and mature. If you have been seriously scarred from past relationships, I'm a great listener with a sympathetic ear, but baggage (yours OR mine) can't dominate the relationship. We all have some; mine is minimal and stays tucked out

*of sight most of the time. Hopefully yours does too! I'm wearing
jeans unless we are going to a wedding or a funeral. If this is
a problem, I'm not your guy. Sorry, but it's a comfort thing.
I am often asked if there is hair under the baseball cap! The
answer is yes.*

He said his name was Dana. I'd never met a man named
Dana before, though one of my college girl friends shares that
name. I studied his picture for a long time. He was tan, tall, and
handsome, with a strong but thin build and a warm, inviting
smile. He was standing next to a small yellow airplane, similar
to the kind that I flew. I liked looking at his picture; it made
me happy. That evening we exchanged a few emails and shared
our phone numbers. I'd learned not to give my phone number
to just anyone I met online, because let's face it, there are a lot of
nut cases out there, and I'd already communicated with a few of
them. But Dana seemed different. He seemed real, and safe. I felt
that because he was a fellow pilot, I could trust him.

Within minutes of sending that email my phone rang. It
was Dana. As we began talking, I took notes about what he was
saying. He was divorced in 2008, had grown weary of the Chicago winters and was looking to move back to the East Coast
to be closer to his mother, who lives in Virginia Beach, and his
brother, who lives in Charlotte. I still have that piece of scrap paper. He said he was working for a restaurant group called Matchbox in D.C. doing maintenance, and that one of the owners was
a friend of his from Chicago, also a pilot. We talked for quite a
while, but it was getting late and I needed to get some rest as
I had to be at the airport early the next morning to fly to New
York with a student. Since I was already booked with students on
Saturday, we agreed to meet at noon on Sunday for a sandwich at
a deli near my house.

I will never forget the first time I saw Dana. I walked into that sandwich shop and looked up at the most handsome, gentle-faced man I'd ever met. He was even taller than I had envisioned from his photo. I thought to myself, "I sure hope this guy is Dana, because if he's not, Dana doesn't stand a chance." It was chilly outside and he was wearing jeans, leather work boots, a tan flannel shirt, a brown leather jacket and a baseball cap with an airplane embroidered on the brim. Then, with a warm smile he reached out his arms and bent down to give me a gentle hug. It was Dana.

From that moment on, I had a strong feeling that this one was going to be different. Dana was polite and a true gentle-man, opening doors and pulling out my chair, but without being condescending. I could tell he was the kind of guy who loved his mother and respected women, and that was very important to me. Knowing I only had an hour and needed to get back to work, he let me eat while he talked about his life as a father and as a pilot. As I listened to Dana tell me the abridged version of his life's story, I looked into his eyes and saw a man who, like me, had suffered intense pain and heartache. He told me some things during that lunch hour that I never imagined anyone would have to go through.

I felt incredible compassion for him, and wanted so badly to let him eat so I could tell him more about myself, but the hour was coming to a close and I had to leave. Dana wrapped up half of his turkey sandwich and, before we parted, gave me another hug and promised to call me again soon. I left hoping he would follow through on that promise.

Chapter 3
A Hole in the Clouds

I had to wait three weeks and three dates for my first kiss from Dana, but it was worth every second. It was just as I'd always envisioned a first kiss should be. This handsome pilot held me in his arms in a quiet, shady spot at the airport and then, when the moment felt just right, gently pressed his lips to mine in a warm embrace. I melted. It was magical, good and innocent. I felt like a teenager again.

We spent the rest of that afternoon at Gravelly Point, one of my favorite parks, overlooking the Potomac River near Washington's Reagan National Airport. We laid in the sun, watching airliners take off and land right over our heads. With each passing week I grew stronger, both physically and emotionally. I was sleeping peacefully through each night for the first time in years and had regained a few much-needed pounds, thanks in part to some very nice meals at the restaurant where Dana worked. We took long walks and hikes together, and spent as much time as we could outdoors. We continued seeing each other regularly and exclusively, with Dana spending nearly every night at my house. By early May he'd vacated his apartment and moved in with me.

Even though we'd only known each other for two months, we'd spent much of that time focusing on understanding each other's history and providing each other with long overdue forgiveness, acceptance and unconditional love. I felt like in those two months, I conducted the most thorough relationship pre-flight inspection of all time. Still, love, like flying, is not without risk, and we both understood that. But we were managing that risk by giving each other the freedom and the time to let go of our pain, without judgment.

We also knew that true love, like flying, really shouldn't be that hard. Being in love shouldn't feel like work, even though loving someone completely requires a great deal of commitment, strength, patience and compassion. I believe there is an essential difference between *loving* someone and *being in love with* someone, and that a healthy marriage needs the latter to thrive, not just survive. If you love someone but don't ache to be with them when they are gone, then I don't think you're in love. On the other hand, passion without love is fleeting and empty, a burst of excitement followed by confusion, pain and loss. But love without passion is incomplete and lonely. And I'm not just talking about physical passion, which naturally ebbs with age and time; I'm talking about intellectual and spiritual passion, the internal forces that drive us through our daily existence and challenge us to seek new experiences, and to learn.

There's an analogy I've often related to students who struggle with the physical act of flying an airplane. Human experience is linear and cumulative. Whenever we are faced with learning a new skill, we try to relate it to something we've done before, to something familiar. A student will often grab the airplane's control yoke and try to use it like the steering wheel of a car to drive the airplane down the runway, when in fact it is the rudder pedals that control the airplane's direction on the ground. The student has to consciously disassociate driving and flying to control the airplane during takeoff and landing. With enough practice and experience, flying becomes as natural as driving, as second nature as being in love. The unique motor skills needed for flying airplanes are summoned instinctively when a seasoned pilot is at the controls, and she feels as if the airplane is an extension of her own body.

That's the way I felt with Dana from the start, as if he were an extension of me, or perhaps in a theoretical physics sense, the me that has existed in a parallel dimension for all eternity. Only through a random gap in the time-space continuum did our paths cross on that early spring day in 2010, forever changing our lives. I have never once questioned our compatibility, and knew very early on in the relationship that we'd spend the rest of our lives together.

Chapter 4

Two Long, Rough Roads

by Dana Holladay

I don't recall being crazy about airplanes as a kid, but I'm certain I was. When I was in my thirties, my mom presented my brother and me with individual scrapbooks of artwork and writing we had produced in our early years. Mine was loaded with drawings of airplanes and stories about flying. However, I do remember when my interest in airplanes became an obsession: It was the day I took my first flying lesson in October 1988.

As my instructor and I took off from the Lake-In-The-Hills Airport northwest of Chicago, I was overcome with emotion. Even though I understood what makes an airplane fly, when that Cessna 152 left the ground it seemed more like magic than physics, and my life was instantly changed. There's a line in the movie *Field of Dreams* that goes, "We just don't recognize the most significant moments of our lives while they're happening." I didn't know it at the time, but that particular moment was the beginning of a journey that would take 22 years and lead me to Meredith, and happiness I never thought possible.

I was 27 years old when I decided to learn how to fly. I had recently moved to the Chicago area from Virginia with my first wife, but didn't know anyone who was a pilot and had no clue where the small airports with flight schools were located. I figured a road map might help, so I borrowed a Rand-McNally road atlas and flipped to the page showing the Chicago metropolitan area. The small airports were depicted with little black airplane symbols, and there were two within a 30-minute drive of my house, Campbell Airport and Lake-In-The-Hills Airport. I took an introductory flight at Campbell and then visited Lake-In-The-Hills, where I signed up for lessons because the rates there were slightly lower. At the time, I knew very little about small airplanes or what was involved in learning how to fly. Like Meredith, I trained in a two-seat Cessna 152 and I remember asking my instructor as we walked up to it if it was a Piper Cub. I couldn't see his face, as I was trailing him by several steps, but I'm certain he rolled his eyes and muttered something like, "Geez! Another day-one student pilot! I can't wait to move on to an airline job!"

I reminisce often about those early days in my aviation career. It's not that they're not all special in their own way, but nothing compares to the emotions that flow during your first lesson, or when you solo for the first time, or the day you pass the flight test and earn the right to call yourself a private pilot. When I started flying, I wasn't interested in investing time and money on advanced ratings. I just wanted to be able to rent a plane and escape the earthbound stress of daily life, take a friend up now and then, and perhaps buy or build my own airplane someday. It is often said that life is what happens while you're busy making other plans, and mine is no exception. Over the next 11 years, I would end up adding several ratings to that private pilot certificate, all the while having no clue they would be the key to finding Meredith.

My path to those advanced ratings turned out to be a bit circuitous. Soon after I passed my private pilot practical test, I joined the Westosha Flying Club at the Westosha Airport in

Wilmot, Wisconsin. A couple of years later I started working on my instrument rating, which is typically the next rung on the pilot ladder. Without an instrument rating, you're not allowed to fly in the clouds, so your flying is more limited with regard to weather conditions. Initially, I found instrument training to be a major challenge for two reasons. First, I spent most of the time staring only at the instrument panel, wearing a view-limiting device over my face so I could learn what it's like to fly in the clouds with no visual reference to the outside world. It was disorienting and often led to vertigo and mental fatigue, which wasn't much fun. Second, I was flying with one of the most burned-out instructors I've ever known and he couldn't have cared less about me or my progress. His training was inefficient and costly in terms of both time and money.

After several months of this I decided to put instrument training on hold for a while. I stopped training for well over a year and almost didn't continue. But I knew earning an instrument rating would sharpen my flying skills, and I like to finish what I start, so I asked one of the other club instructors, Tom Horton, if he could help. Tom agreed to work with me and by May 1995 we had completed my training and I passed the practical test. I was so happy that I gave Tom a two-hundred-dollar tip for getting me through it.

I can't say enough about the influence Tom has had on my flying career. He's a few years older than I am and has been a flight instructor with the Westosha Flying Club since he was 19. He's not only very knowledgable, but also laid back and extremely patient, and can say more with five words than most of us can say with 50. He'll often slip something into a lesson, like a simulated landing gear or engine temperature problem, in a way that will not only allow the student to sort through it and take action, but also remember the lesson years later.

I was a member of the Westosha Flying Club for over 20 years, which allowed me to observe Tom working with students on literally hundreds of occasions. Often, I would listen in on Tom's lessons, usually hidden out of sight in my cubicle or sitting at the weather terminal at the opposite end of the classroom, so I could learn from the master. Most importantly, I learned from him which things deserve special emphasis and which don't. Every new instructor should have a mentor like Tom Horton and I consider myself extremely lucky to have been able to learn so much from him through the years.

After completing my instrument training, I continued to fly recreationally, logging about 50 hours per year. I even purchased an old single-seat ultralight which amounted to a hang glider with wheels, a seat and an engine that ran pretty well most of the time. Ultralights allow you to fly low and slow, providing a flying experience that can't be matched by planes that fly higher and faster. Low and slow is my favorite kind of flying. There's nothing like flying over the countryside at treetop level, smelling freshly mown grass, feeling the air temperature change between the hills and valleys, and chasing deer and getting outrun by them.

In October 1997, I took my first flight in a Piper Cub, with Tom Horton as my instructor. I had heard many accounts of this venerable little plane over the years, mainly from old-timers who had long since given up flying but couldn't resist hanging out at the airport to wait for the perfect moment to chime in with their favorite flying stories. But I didn't completely understand what all the fuss was about until I actually flew one.

The Cub is a low and slow airplane, much like an ultralight. The most popular model, the J-3, was built between 1937 and 1947 and was the most widely used training airplane of its day. I like that they are mechanically simple with minimal instrumentation. I also like the door and window design, which allows you to fly with both opened wide to provide a mostly unobstructed view of the world. It also allows people on the ground to get a good look at you as you fly overhead, and they'll often wave and can see you waving back. I've never had that happen in any other airplane. If I could fly only one airplane, it would be a Cub. My love affair with the Cub was the main reason Meredith and I eventually chose to purchase one for our trip around the country.

But a lot of things would have to happen before my Cub dream could become a reality. On a cold, rainy Sunday morning in March 2000, I experienced what I can only describe as a stroke of luck followed a few weeks later by a huge leap of faith. I was about to turn 39 and was in a very bad place emotionally, as my first marriage was in a shambles after slowly deteriorating over the course of several years. I was also working for a company that by all accounts was a sinking ship, so I was suffering from quite a bit of stress and anxiety.

One of my routine escapes from this ugly reality was eating at a local diner, where I could sit by myself, enjoy an inexpensive meal, ponder life, and try to figure out my next move. I would usually bring an aviation magazine to read, but sometimes I'd buy a newspaper, as I did that morning. After finishing breakfast, I decided to see if there were any interesting job listings in the classifieds. I had never searched for a job in the newspaper and didn't have much hope that I would find one there, but it seemed like a good way to kill time while finishing my last cup of coffee. I skimmed page after page of jobs that had no appeal to me whatsoever, and then there it was, a little ad that contained the word aviation. It simply read, "Sales/Management position in the aviation industry. Send resume to H. David Huser," followed by the address. I remember telling myself not to get too excited in case it didn't pan out. I circled the ad, folded the paper, dropped a tip on the table, and drove home to dust off my resume, which I mailed with a cover letter the next day.

After a month went by and I didn't hear anything, I assumed the position had been filled and forgot all about it. Then I received a phone call from Dave Huser, one of the owners of American Flyers, a nationwide flight school with a great reputation in the flight training business. He was looking for a salesman for their flight school at what is now called Chicago Executive Airport (formerly Palwaukee), which was not far from my house. We talked for several minutes and he said I sounded like the kind of guy he was looking for, and that he'd like to meet in person.

I told him the job sounded interesting and thanked him for the call, but also told him that I'd changed my mind about switching jobs. I'd attended a motivational meeting at work a couple weeks after I mailed him my resume, and had come to believe the sinking ship had plugged its holes. On top of that, I assumed that working at American Flyers would involve a pay cut and I hated the idea of trying to sell that idea to my wife. I knew there was no way she would be happy with that news, even if it meant I'd be working in an industry that I loved and would be much happier there. Fortunately for me, Dave was not fazed by my change of heart and asked me to keep him in mind. I remember feeling encouraged by the fact that he was still interested in me after I told him I was no longer interested in the position.

For the next couple of weeks I couldn't stop thinking about the possibility of working at an airport. I also couldn't stop thinking about how miserable I was and concluded that if the offer still stood, I should meet with Dave and learn more about the position. That meeting would occur on a Saturday a few weeks later. I had reserved one of our flying club airplanes for the day to give free rides to kids as part of the Experimental Aircraft Association's Young Eagles program. We completed the Young Eagles flights just before noon, so I decided to call Dave to see if he was available. Because it was a Saturday, I didn't expect him to be working, but he was. Dave's office was almost an hour away by car, but 15 minutes by plane. I told him it would be convenient for me to fly down that day if he had time for a meeting. I also warned him that I was dressed in shorts, a t-shirt and sneakers, not exactly the best attire for an interview. He said he didn't care how I was dressed, and I told him I'd be there as soon as possible.

Thirty minutes later I was sitting in his office getting details about American Flyers and the job opening at Palwaukee. We talked for about 45 minutes and I told him I was interested in the position. He stated that before he could offer me the job, I would have to interview with two additional board members, so I returned three days later and, after another interview, was offered and accepted the position for the Palwaukee location. I was so excited I felt like I was going to explode. Then my thoughts turned to breaking the news to my wife. She had just left for a month-long trip to Europe with her parents, and by the time she returned from her trip I had been working at American Flyers for about two weeks. When she found out what I had done, she wasn't happy, but in time realized it was for the better.

From my first day on the job, I loved it and felt better than I had in years. I shadowed Dave for almost a month at the Du-Page office before he transferred me to Palwaukee. That location had been struggling, but within a few months we were able to turn things around and I settled comfortably into my position, thanks in large part to Dave's patience and guidance. He not only taught me how to run a flight school, but also how to manage people.

One of the benefits of working at a flight school is virtually unlimited access to planes and instructors. Dave recognized my hard work by allowing me to train for my commercial and flight instructor certificates when the schedule allowed. I studied at home, flew when I could and earned my commercial pilot certificate in March 2001, just a few months before Meredith would take her first flight lesson. A few weeks later I started working toward a flight instructor certificate. The preparation for the flight instructor test is grueling and requires a lot of reading, a minimum of two knowledge tests, and a practical test. You also have to learn to fly from the right seat as opposed to the left, where the pilot normally sits. This is like learning to write with the wrong hand, except there's no eraser if you make a mistake.

At first it felt like I was learning to fly all over again, but practice quickly took care of that. I had been teaching people how to fly radio-controlled model airplanes for almost 10 years, so I was comfortable with verbalizing while flying, something that is very difficult for most budding flight instructors. And because I had been running a flight school for a year and a half, most of the knowledge required was firmly locked in my brain. By December 2001, I was signed off by my instructor to take the test. The examiner and I flew for about an hour and a half and just like that, I was a newly minted flight instructor. What a long, crazy road it had been to get to that point.

It's rare that someone gets to earn a living doing what he or she truly loves, but the next nine years would find me doing just that. On the day after I passed my flight instructor test I started teaching in the club planes at Westosha. This started out as a part-time endeavor since I was still managing the flight school at Palwaukee. I had several friends who wanted to learn to fly and had been waiting for me to pass the flight instructor test so they could train with me. I have always been passionate about teaching people how to fly and I pour my heart and soul into it. I'm also very efficient, so my students were completing their training as fast as their schedules and money would allow. I gained a reputation in the area as a fun, no-nonsense, results-oriented instructor. By spring of 2003, I was so busy instructing that I realized I might be able to make a living at it alone. I hated the idea of leaving American Flyers, but after a couple of heart-to-heart conversations with Dave Huser, he agreed that my real passion was in the cockpit and not behind a desk, so I resigned from American Flyers and began instructing full-time at Westosha.

Most people learn to fly in their spare time after work, so that meant teaching in the evening and on weekends. I was having so much fun that most of the time I didn't know what day it was, and didn't really care. When I wasn't instructing, I was ferrying and test flying airplanes all around the country. The ferry flights were mostly for people who had purchased airplanes that were far away and didn't have the time or confidence to pick them up themselves. I crossed the Rocky Mountains several times, got to see the Grand Canyon, had partial or complete engine failures in flight on several occasions, and had two flights in unstable homebuilt airplanes that almost ended in catastrophe.

Fortunately, I was able to land safely each time. I learned a lot about flying from those emergencies, and there's no doubt they made me a better pilot.

I stayed very busy flying until about a year after the economy tanked in 2008. With the downturn in the economy my workload dropped significantly, and I limped along for another year or so barely making ends meet. It became painfully obvious that my days of making a living flying little airplanes were rapidly coming to an end, and I would have to pursue another line of work.

When I was with American Flyers I worked briefly with a guy named Mark Neal. Mark is a pilot who came into my office in the summer of 2001 to inquire about flight instructor training. I asked him what his career objective was and he said he wasn't sure, but he hadn't flown since the day he got his commercial certificate many years prior and wanted to get back into flying. I had been looking to hire someone to help with operations and asked Mark if he was interested in the position. He said yes and within a few weeks was onboard, but we'd only worked together for about three months when the 9/11 attacks occurred. The aftermath brought the flight training industry to its knees and Mark was a victim of the inevitable cutbacks that followed.

This turned out to be fortunate for Mark, as he wound up moving to Washington, D.C. and with his brother and two other partners, built a very successful restaurant business called Matchbox. Mark and I kept in touch over the years and would always see each other at the annual air show in Oshkosh, Wisconsin, or when I would pass through D.C. on my way to visit my mom in Virginia. Every time I'd ask him how his business was doing, he'd tell me about record sales and how he could use more help. I'd joke that someday I might move back east and may need to ask him for a job. His reply was always the same: "We could really use more help with our restaurant maintenance. Just say the word and the job is yours."

I had been thinking about moving for many years, but had made a promise to my daughter, Nikki, that I wouldn't leave until she had graduated from high school. Nikki's graduation and my divorce occurred in 2008, but I still wasn't ready to leave Chicago. I had spent several years building my instructing business and customer base, and knew that if I moved, it would be very difficult to start over in a new location. But the economic crash that fall forced my hand. The flight training business slowed significantly and I limped along for a little over a year, instructing when I could and supplementing my income by doing odd jobs here and there. By the end of 2009, I was in debt for the first time in many years and talking with Mark seriously about moving to D.C. That was a very difficult time. I had lived in the Chicago area for over 20 years and loved everything about the Midwest except the winter weather. Leaving Chicago meant walking away from a job I truly loved, but in early January 2010, I accepted a position as director of maintenance with Matchbox and started tying up loose ends at home in preparation for the move.

I was very stressed out about the change and decided to drive to Charlotte to spend a few days with my brother, Marc, prior to heading to D.C. Marc has always been a good sounding board when it comes to major decisions and I felt the need to spend some time with him to talk about where my life was headed. I arrived at his house in early February and the next day we found ourselves watching a weather forecast that predicted a massive snowstorm would hit the Mid-Atlantic region over the weekend. This would turn out to be the same storm I'd later learn compelled Meredith to join Match.com.

By late Saturday, many areas north of Charlotte were buried in over two feet of snow. I remember thinking to myself, "No problem. It's Saturday. Surely by Monday morning, the main roads will be plowed and I'll be able to get to D.C. and start my new job." I woke up Monday morning and called Mark to check on the road conditions there. He told me the city was paralyzed and no one was going anywhere by car. The Washington area wasn't equipped to deal with the amount of snow that had fallen and many of the snowplows were getting stuck. To make matters worse, a second snowstorm hit the region the next day and I wasn't able to make it up to D.C. for several more days.

Mark had a vacant apartment over his garage, so I was able to live there for a couple of months while I settled into the new job and searched for another place to live. About six weeks after arriving in D.C., I was feeling rather lonely and decided to start dating again. I had no interest in getting remarried and was hoping to find someone who was comfortable with that. I had tried online dating in Chicago after my first marriage ended, met some nice women, and went out on several dates, but none of them resulted in a serious relationship. It was nice to get out now and then, but also frustrating going through the effort with not much to show for it. Nonetheless, I felt that online dating was the most efficient way to find someone with whom I shared similar interests, so one evening I logged onto Match.com, the same site I had used in Chicago.

Even though I entered a somewhat limited search by geographic area and age, about 400 photos came up. I scanned the photos for quite a while and came across the one Meredith had posted. I was mesmerized. It was a photo of a beautiful woman flying a small airplane with a smile on her face that told me she was in her element. Not only that, she was flying from the right seat, so I was almost certain she was a flight instructor. I remember telling myself not to get too excited. After all, the only thing I could infer from this photo was that we had a mutual love of flying. That alone won't sustain a relationship, so I had to find out more about her.

My status on Match.com was inactive at that time so I couldn't read anyone's profile. All I could see were the photos with screen names, ages, and locations. I pulled out my credit card and activated my account to read what Meredith had to say. After reading it no less than three times, I couldn't wait to speak to her. Reading her profile was like reading something I might have written about myself. I sent her a brief email to see if she'd like to talk, and two days later we met for lunch at a sandwich shop near her house.

Chapter 5
The Happy Movie

I will always remember those first few months of getting to know Dana by a phrase I coined with him, "my happy movie." I'd tell Dana that everything we did together was a new scene in my happy movie, the one I could replay in my mind to smile instead of dwelling on the nightmares of the past. In a very short time we'd developed a foundation of positive, common experiences that we both could rely on and call our own.

One of those happy movie scenes unfolded on April 28, 2010, the night Dana and I attended a company party to celebrate the opening of a new restaurant. It was the first time we'd met his coworkers as a couple. As we walked in Dana greeted Mark's brother and business partner Ty Neal, and Ty's young daughter. She was wearing a flowery dress and had a sparkly pink butterfly painted on her cheek. She recognized Dana instantly, and the butterfly stretched its wings with her smile. He scooped her up in his arms and placed her on his shoulders, bouncing her up and down as if she were his own. The sheer joy on both of their faces was intoxicating. I found myself frozen in a moment of blissful suspended animation and thought, "This man is going to be the father of my child someday."

It had been many years since I'd entertained the notion of being a mother, but when I saw Dana standing there smiling with this bubbly little girl on his shoulders, something inside of me changed. I felt as though the lights in an old house had been switched on after years of darkness. I wanted to marry him and make a baby with him, but I was 38 and he was almost 50, with a 20-year-old daughter from his first marriage. I wondered if a man who was changing diapers while I was still in college would be willing and able to do it again, for me, now.

I kept those thoughts to myself for a few days, letting them take root in my mind. I daydreamed about Dana and I as parents, taking our child on his or her first flight in our airplane. The vision seemed so tangible to me that one night after dinner, as we lay on the sofa watching television, I told Dana how I felt seeing him hold that little girl at the party. I told him how it awakened a part of me that I thought had died. We'd only been dating a month, but I thought I'd better let him know how I was feeling up front, in case he decided to bolt.

Before I even had the chance to ask him what he thought of this, he held me and said that if I ever wanted to have a baby, he would be thrilled to be the father. However, there was just one small technical detail to overcome: Dana had undergone a vasectomy in 2008.

"But it's completely reversible," he said, in the same calm, confident tone he uses when talking on the radio in the airplane. "It's just a minor plumbing repair. No big deal."

Plumbing? No big deal? I lay there stunned and amazed and wondered, who is this man and what planet is he from? Each day with Dana brought me new insight into the meaning of unconditional love. During those first few months of dating we often felt like we were in a time-warp, making up for lost years. We talked openly and freely about our future, but never at the expense of the present. Neither of us wanted to make that mistake again, of letting days and weeks and years pass by without enjoying the time we had together. Life was marching forward in a positive new direction, and we each felt secure knowing that our darkest days were far behind us.

Flying together became a wonderful obsession and we sought every opportunity to get in an airplane, or at least spend time hanging out at an airport. On May 7, 2010, I flew to Atlanta with a student in his airplane to attend an aviation safety seminar. My aunt and her family live in Atlanta, so I thought it would be a great opportunity to visit with them, too. Dana was also flying that weekend, ferrying a small seaplane from Vero Beach, Florida to Chicago for its owner. Atlanta is about halfway between those two cities, so Dana decided to stop in to see me, refuel and spend the night at my aunt's house. I would make that ferry flight with Dana two more times before the owner sold the plane in the fall of 2011, and those wonderful trips were part of what inspired us to embark on our epic cross-country flight in the summer of 2012.

I snuck out of the seminar early on Saturday afternoon so I could be waiting at the Peachtree-Dekalb Airport when Dana landed. After a short snack break, Dana asked me if I'd like to go up for a ride. Watching him check the fuel and oil, and then pull the plane into position on the ramp as if it were a child's toy, was incredibly erotic. He helped me into the back seat, then he climbed into the front seat and started the engine.

That airplane, like our Cub, was built in the tandem configuration, where the pilot and passenger sit in line with, rather than next to, one another. I will never forget that flight because it was the first of many times I had the pleasure of studying Dana from the back seat of an airplane: the beautiful tan skin on his neck, the contour of his strong shoulders, and the way his soft brown hair glistens in the sun to reveal hints of amber. That view reminded me of the many hours I'd already spent riding with Dana on the back of his motorcycle, with my arms wrapped around his fit waist, watching his strong hands and arms navigate twists and turns in the road, all while breathing in the intoxicating smell of his warm skin.

I loved hearing his voice on the radio, a voice that hinted both of the two decades he'd spent living in the upper Midwest, and of his childhood years in the Tidewater region of Virginia. When he called for his taxi clearance, I knew I was in the hands of a true professional. He earned my respect as a pilot before we ever left the ground.

I was awed by his stick-and-rudder skill and the smooth, effortless way he handled the controls. It was as if he was born knowing how to do this. He seemed completely at peace in the sky, flying with the grace and ease of a bird. The plane could have exploded and crashed in a fiery ball that day and I would have gone down with a smile on my face, content that I'd finally experienced true happiness during my last moments on earth.

When Dana took off at sunrise the next morning to complete his trip to Chicago, I stood in the airport parking lot and watched his lights disappear into the indigo twilight sky. I couldn't wait to see him again, back at home in Maryland, later that night.

By the week of my divorce hearing in July 2010, Dana and I were ready for a break and looking forward to what for each of us has become a summertime tradition: traveling to Oshkosh, Wisconsin, for EAA AirVenture, the world's largest and the country's most widely attended aviation festival. On the morning after I legally reclaimed my birth name, Dana and I loaded our camping gear into my flying club's Cessna 182 and headed west to the place where we could spend an entire week in the sun, surrounded by cornfields and airplanes.

We arrived at the show to find the airfield soaked in puddles and mud, but fortunately, Dana's new boss, Mark, had staked out a camping spot for us on high ground, so we were dry and comfortable in our tent that night. It was the first time Dana and I had slept under the stars together. I thought to myself that life could not get much better, but I was wrong.

Just before sunrise the next day, Dana and I went for a walk to one of his favorite spots, Compass Hill, overlooking the fairgrounds. It's a place where Dana spent many quiet moments over the years, contemplating his life and the swift passage of time. A sculpture at the top of the hill features life-sized bronze statues of a young family, with a boy holding a toy airplane skyward.

It seemed to me that Dana was rather fidgety as we walked quietly, hand in hand, to the hill. The sun had just begun to crest the summit when Dana took me in his arms, asked me to close my eyes, and slipped a diamond ring onto my left hand. I knew instantly what it was when I felt it on my skin, but I could hardly believe it was happening. I lost all control of my emotions and began crying and laughing simultaneously, and felt dizzy from hyperventilation. Dana held me tight so I wouldn't fall down.

After I regained feeling in my extremities and we had a chance to absorb the moment, we walked back to camp to tell our friends the good news. In a way, we were just as stunned as some of them were. In four short months, our lives had turned completely around. Just when we thought we were hopelessly lost in the clouds, we found direction in each other. We were flying the airplane, and in a steady climb.

Later that morning, as I sat at a picnic table with Dana and his friends eating Wisconsin's famous fried cheese curds, I couldn't stop staring at the beautiful, sparkling ring on my hand. I told Dana that I truly would have been happy with something simpler or nothing at all, but he insisted that I deserved a nice ring. I had long since forgotten what it felt like to be so selflessly appreciated and respected, and though I hated to admit it, Dana's gift was a revalidation of my self worth. I allowed myself the pleasure of feeling desirable and sexy, walking around the fairgrounds hand in hand with the tall, fit, handsome, rock-star pilot who would soon be my husband.

That afternoon while watching the daily air show, we checked our calendars and decided to have the wedding on a Saturday in October, just three months away. Being the jeans and t-shirts kind of people that we are, we saw no reason to spend lots of time and money planning a fancy wedding when all we really wanted was a small, casual party with our family and a few close friends. We called our families to tell them the good news, and I immediately got busy planning logistics, using my iPhone to search for potential venues for the event.

My original idea was to have the wedding outdoors at a rental house overlooking the Hudson River in New York, near where I grew up, so my elderly grandmother would be able to attend. However, all of the venues we liked were way out of our price range. So with my family's consent we decided to have the wedding in Laytonsville, Maryland at Davis Airport, a small airport located just a few miles down the road from the main airpark in Gaithersburg where I learned to fly. We'd visit my grandmother a week or two afterward, bringing her plenty of videos and photos. She was fine with it.

We offered the manager of Davis Airport a donation toward his budding flight school in exchange for use of the hangar, which included a pair of rest rooms, a full-size refrigerator and a dozen picnic tables. The airport's parklike setting, surrounded by trees with a picket fence and a small pond near the east end of the runway, was idyllic.

The three months between the engagement and the wedding passed quickly, as we were still busy painting and cleaning up the house before putting it on the market. Earlier that summer, when I'd told my first husband about Dana, I'd agreed to let him take custody of our dog, who we'd adopted as a puppy back in 2001. Dana saw how badly I missed having a dog around the house, though, so the week after we returned from Oshkosh we went to the Washington Animal Rescue League and adopted a puppy of our own. He was a four-month-old foxhound mutt, skinny and scared, and completely adorable. We named him Booey, after Booeymonger, the sandwich shop where we had our first date.

My parents, Nick and Gail, drove down from New York a few days before the wedding to help us with preparations, which were minimal. At home we prepared a simple lunch of pulled rotisserie chicken and gravy, pasta salad, green salad, bread, and fruit. My college roommate Alison Bennett baked us a fabulous wedding cake adorned with a small model airplane. Booey was the designated ring bearer, though he was still too much of a crazy puppy to handle the responsibility. My father was in charge of Booey during the ceremony and made sure the little guy didn't eat our rings.

While our friends and family brought the food to Davis and got the coffee brewing for lunch, Dana and I were five miles away at the Montgomery County Airpark in Gaithersburg, preparing to climb into the cockpit of our wedding limo, the very same Cessna 182 we had flown out to Wisconsin that summer for the air show. I wore black jeans and a red silk button-down sweater with a rose petal print tank top, matching beaded shoes, and my old black leather jacket. Dana was wearing black jeans and an ivory button-down collared shirt, complemented by a brand new pair of black Chuck Taylor high-top sneakers, his favorite.

It was a sunny, crisp fall morning and the leaves had just started to change color. We couldn't have asked for a prettier day to get married, except the weather forecast called for very gusty northwest winds all day long. Our "Plan B" in case of bad weather was to drive to Davis, but we had our hearts set on flying to our wedding. Even though we'd already flown many hours together, that short flight was going to be a critical test of our ability to work effectively as a team and make sound and safe decisions as a flight crew.

The first decision was to leave Booey on the ground at Davis with my dad. We really wanted Booey to fly with us, but thought the turbulence might make him nervous and sick even on such a short flight. I was also a little worried about my ability to land in a stiff crosswind in front of dozens of friends and family members on my wedding day. Since Dana had more than double the flight hours I did, with lots more experience landing on short, narrow airstrips, I asked him if he'd be willing to act as pilot in command of our wedding limo flight. He agreed, and promised me that if for any reason he wasn't comfortable with the conditions at Davis, he'd abort and return to Gaithersburg where the landing would be easier.

Gaithersburg's single runway is oriented toward the northwest (320 degrees on the compass), so there would be little crosswind component. The runway at Davis is oriented toward the west (260 degrees), where Dana would face a challenging crosswind from the right. Plus, Davis' runway is less than half as wide and half as long as the one at Gaithersburg, making it even more difficult to keep the wheels on the pavement when the wind is trying to blow the airplane sideways.

I buckled into the copilot seat clutching my home-made bouquet and Dave, our official wedding mascot. Dave is a plush toy elephant we'd outfitted with a parachute. The elephant is a metaphor we used for the challenges we faced in dealing with the sale of the house. "Fixing the house is like eating an elephant," Dana would say to me when I'd get anxious about the sale. "We just have to keep taking little bites and eventually it'll be gone." Dave and his parachute now live in our guest bedroom, encouraging us to keep moving forward whenever we start to feel overloaded by life's challenges.

The plan was for Dana to fly about 500 feet over the runway at Davis and then slow down so I could open my window and launch Dave, ushering our arrival. It was amazing to look out and see everyone standing there by the hangar waiting for us to land. Dana handled the landing easily, as I knew he would. As he made his final descent toward the runway, I thought to myself that the next time we'd get into a plane together, we'd be married.

The landing approach was extremely turbulent, but Dana got us safely down onto the narrow, lumpy runway with plenty of room to spare. Watching him land the airplane with such skill was an incredible rush for me. With everyone standing around taking pictures of us, I felt like a celebrity arriving on a private jet for a movie debut.

We are not at all religious, but we still needed a licensed official to oversee the wedding ceremony and sign the marriage certificate. A pilot friend had suggested I contact the local Civil Air Patrol chaplain, whom he said would probably be happy to participate in our civil ceremony at the airport. The chaplain respected our wishes and, after a brief welcome and introduction to our guests gathered around the pond near the approach end of the runway we'd just landed on, he turned the attention to Dana and I and invited us to read the vows we'd written.

Dana insisted I go first. Much like my Match.com profile, my letter to him didn't take very long to write, because the thoughts flowed out of my brain so effortlessly. I brought along a printed copy, not trusting my ability to memorize and recall the entire thing from start to finish. Speaking in front of groups of people has always made me anxious, and I didn't want to mess up this very important moment. So I pulled a folded page from my pocket, looked at Dana with a smile and began.

> Dana, when you came into my life, you gave me the greatest gift—hope. Hope that life can be better, not in a decade or when I have a million dollars in my pocket, but today, right here and right now, with whatever we have available to us. All I had to do was open up my heart, let you in and live in the moment.
>
> You gently, patiently and lovingly stood by my side and provided a safe place for me to let go of the past and embrace the present. When I cried you held me, and when I laughed you encouraged me to laugh some more. You never judged me or questioned me. You just saw the best in me, and gave me the freedom to see the best in myself.
>
> Every moment with you now is so precious. I wake up every morning excited and optimistic knowing that you are there to share it with me. If I were to die today, I'd leave this world content in the knowledge that I'd found my soul's true companion. Dana, I believe that you have always been with me in spirit, and I will be forever thankful that we finally found each other.
>
> I promise you that I will do my very best to protect, respect and love you with all my heart every day we have together. I love you so much and I am so glad to be sharing this life with you now.

"Do you blame her for having a cheat sheet?" Dana laughed as he wiped a tear from his eye. Then, he spoke these words to me, which he had typed on his iPhone and read aloud to himself every day for a week until he had them memorized.

Mer, there is no way I can put into words how much I love you or what you mean to me, but I don't need to, because you know. I knew soon after we met that we would spend the rest of our lives together, and to see your excitement when I asked you to marry me was one of the greatest moments of my life.

Two long, rough roads intersected when we found each other. Every twist and turn in those roads led us here, deeply in love and getting married in the presence of our families and closest friends. There are few things in life that are certain, but I can tell you this beyond the shadow of a doubt. As long as I am alive, you'll never be alone, or unloved, or unappreciated. I will always be there for you. You've made me happier than I ever thought possible, and I couldn't be prouder to be your husband and best friend.

Chapter 6
Managing Expectations

After the wedding, Dana and I felt an increased urgency to sell my house and move into a place of our own. By late January, we had found an agreeable buyer and closed the deal on February 28, 2011. After paying off the primary mortgage, the home equity loan and closing costs, I walked away with about $1,500—a fraction of what I'd originally hoped for, but not bad considering the depressed state of the national economy and real estate market.

Dana and I spent the winter looking for a new place to live, and found a modest but well-maintained, three-bedroom Cape Cod for rent a few miles north of the old house. We moved in and immediately felt more comfortable in our new neighborhood. A group of quiet, friendly young women lived next door with a sweet old pit bull mutt that immediately befriended young Booey. Across the street lived a single mom, her son and their chocolate lab puppy. Everyone on the block who was home that Saturday greeted us as we were unloading the moving van, and we made several new friends. It was a huge relief.

With the last remnant of my first marriage behind me, Dana and I were able to focus on our goals and dreams as a couple, which included trying to conceive a child. I was 38 and I knew the end of my child-bearing days was rapidly approaching, but I was encouraged by the constant stream of reports from high school and college classmates who were announcing their first, second and even third babies. I visited my gynecologist for a check-up and was referred to a local fertility center for an evaluation. All of my blood work and other tests indicated my plumbing was working just fine, and that my eggs were still very healthy. The doctors saw no reason why we shouldn't be able to conceive naturally, but they cautioned us that given my "advanced maternal age" I shouldn't get my hopes up either. Statistics show that the odds of a woman getting pregnant decrease dramatically after age 35 and after 40, it's about as likely as winning the lottery. Well not exactly, but that's what it felt like to me.

Even though time was working against us, there was still hope. So in January 2011, we met with one of the most reputable surgeons in the area who specializes in the vasectomy reversal procedure. The $11,000 surgery would be a big step for us, emotionally and financially. We didn't expect the fee to be covered by Dana's health insurance, and took out a consumer line of credit to pay for it. To our amazement, the reversal was fully covered by Dana's insurance. The alternative to the surgery, in vitro fertilization (IVF), would not have been covered by either of our insurance plans, was considerably more expensive than the reversal and came with consequences and risks that we decided were not acceptable to us for a variety of reasons. Although our chances of getting pregnant with IVF were considerably higher than with the reversal, IVF was a "one shot deal" whereas a successful reversal meant virtually unlimited attempts to get pregnant, and to do so naturally. With both of us in good health, we decided that the reversal was the best option, and scheduled Dana's surgery for early April, at an outpatient center north of Baltimore.

I was so nervous the night before the surgery that I had trouble sleeping for the first time since we met. I set an alarm for 5:15 a.m. but tossed and turned all night thinking about Dana and hoping we were making the right decision, not about wanting to have a baby, but for his health. I knew he was in relatively good shape for 50 and that a vasectomy reversal is not as big a deal as, say, open-heart or brain surgery, but still, it involved putting him under general anesthesia and cutting him open. My mind raced with doomsday scenarios: What if the doctor sneezes and the knife slips out of her hand during a critical moment? What if Dana has a bad reaction to the sedative and never wakes up? If anything went wrong and he died I could never forgive myself. What would I tell his family? They didn't know about the surgery because Dana wanted to wait to tell them what we'd done until after I became pregnant, in case our efforts were unsuccessful.

About four hours after we arrived, the surgeon came out and told me the procedure was complete and that Dana was recovering, and I could see him in a few minutes. Initial tests showed the plumbing job was a success, but it would be several months before we'd know for sure whether his swim team was ready for serious competition. As I'd feared, Dana suffered a severe reaction to the anesthesia and was very sick for several days after the surgery. Still, through it all he was cracking jokes and smiling and reassuring me it would all be okay. A week later we were back to our normal work routine, though it would be several weeks before Dana was fully recovered from the surgery.

Dana's prediction that I would be pregnant by Oshkosh that year didn't come true. I imagined coming home from Wisconsin with a baby bump to trump the sparkling diamond engagement ring I returned with the year before. I suppose it was a completely unrealistic expectation. The surgeon said it could take up to a year for us to conceive after the surgery. So we kept trying, and kept hoping.

Summer turned to fall, and with each passing week we grew restless to plan the trip we'd each dreamed of for years before we met: taking a couple of months off to fly a small airplane around the United States. We still had hope that within a year we'd be parents, and we felt attempting the trip with a newborn baby in tow would be too difficult. Delaying the trip for another 10-15 years, when Dana would be ready to retire, didn't seem like a reasonable option, either. What if our health deteriorated and we lost our ability to fly? A million things could happen in that span of time. We had to get started, and soon.

Chapter 7
The Results Business

With our minds made up to launch on our around-the-country flight in the summer of 2012, we began shopping for an airplane. Dana had previously owned a share in a Cub and really missed flying that little plane low and slow over the Wisconsin countryside. The Cub, like the seaplane Dana flew to Atlanta, has two seats in tandem configuration, weighs about 725 pounds, and has a cruise speed of about 75 miles per hour. It's developed a cult following among aviation purists for its simplicity and uniquely identifiable school-bus-yellow paint scheme with a black lightning bolt design near the engine compartment and the classic bear cub icon on the tail.

Nostalgia and fun factor notwithstanding, we also felt the Cub would be an excellent platform for taking photos during the trip, since the door opens wide to offer substantially better visibility than most other light airplanes. The Cub also burns relatively little fuel, about five gallons per hour.

We found a beautiful 1938 J-3 Cub for sale near Orlando, Florida, with a 12-gallon auxiliary fuel tank providing the additional range we'd need to comfortably traverse the mountains and deserts out west. With rebuilt wings, a recently overhauled 90-horsepower engine, and a nearly flawless paint job, this Cub fit our mission perfectly. By Christmas we'd reached an agreement with the seller and made plans to bring the plane home to Maryland over the New Year weekend, weather permitting.

What many non-pilots don't realize is that owning a small, simple airplane like a Cub does not cost *that* much more than owning a large sport utility vehicle or luxury car. Also, airplanes hold their value far better than cars. The annual insurance and maintenance for our Cub was about the same as for our used Honda Odyssey minivan, and they both got about the same gas mileage.

We ordered a wall-sized planning chart of the United States and laid it out on the coffee table one evening, placing little sticky notes over the approximate locations that would define our route. The trip was starting to take shape. Since our Cub could fly about 250 miles between fuel stops, we figured we'd need to make at least 35 stops along the route, which would cover approximately 8,000 miles. Realistically, though, we planned to make many more stops than that to fly shorter, more comfortable legs, do a bit of sightseeing and dodge bad weather we'd inevitably encounter along the way.

The big question was, how were we going to pay for an eight-week joyride around the country in our new old airplane? Assuming nothing went wrong along the way—we didn't get sick and the airplane didn't break down—we estimated it would cost about $10,000 for fuel, food, hotel, and other expenses, not to mention two months of lost income. Dana had decided to resign from Matchbox and return to flight instruction after we returned from our trip, because he missed teaching and realized that taking two months off from his job at the restaurant wasn't going to work out.

We were not independently wealthy, we were too young to retire, and the economy was still shaky. Some people said we were insane to think of leaving a comfortable existence to chase a dream, but we knew that the time to do this was never going to be perfect, and we weren't getting any younger. Besides, with all of our credit cards paid off, my old house sold, and Dana's house in Chicago rented out, we really couldn't think of a reason not to do it. Our savings would pay for nearly all of our trip expenses, and we hoped to get a few sponsors from within our aviation network to help supplement the cost of fuel and overnight hangar space. Dana and I have always said, "We're in the results business," and it was time to put that to the test.

Chapter 8

Trusting Science and Nature

We visited my parents in New York for the Thanksgiving holiday and told them about our trip plans. They were genuinely happy for us and agreed to watch Booey while we were gone, which saved us hundreds of dollars in pet sitter fees. The weather was unseasonably warm that weekend, so Dana and I went for a long hike along the Hudson River with my dad and Booey.

My dad and I have always shared a special bond, and aviation has always been the glue that's held our friendship together. We wrap our Christmas presents in expired aeronautical charts and never get bored talking about the weather. In the years during my childhood when he had a little extra money, Dad would rent the old Cherokee he learned to fly in so we could go bore holes in the sky over the Hudson River, flying past Manhattan and circling the Statue of Liberty. Hiking along the Hudson always reminds me of those early flights together, just me and Dad, enjoying the sky.

When I earned my instrument rating in 2004, Dad was the first person who agreed to fly with me in the clouds. He and I flew to Oshkosh that summer in the same plane Dana and I used as our wedding limo. Watching Dad and Dana walking together along the river, talking about flying, pilot to pilot, during that hike made me feel my life had finally come full circle.

Dad attended the same high school I did, Nyack High School, and by all accounts was a happy-go-lucky, all-American kid, listening to rock and roll music, working on cars, sneaking into Manhattan on the bus and playing varsity football. He was always fascinated with airplanes and recalled a particularly inspirational early childhood encounter with Russian-American aviation pioneer Igor Sikorsky, who was a family acquaintance through his mother's association with Alexandra Tolstoy, the daughter of the Russian author of *War and Peace*, Leo Tolstoy. Sikorsky became famous not only for his helicopters but also for designing the flying boats Pan Am used for transatlantic airline service during the 1930s. He died in 1972, a few months after I was born.

Dad attended the State University of New York at Buffalo for two years before being drafted into the U.S. Army to support the Vietnam war effort. He elected instead to volunteer for enlistment into the U.S. Air Force because he wanted to be involved in some way with aviation. He arrived in Saigon in September 1969 and was assigned to the 483rd Tactical Combat Support Group, initially stationed at Vung Tau, about 50 miles southeast of Saigon. He was there until July 1970, when the squadron was moved north to Cam Ranh Bay. Dad worked as an aircraft engine technician with flying status, which meant he did maintenance and flew as part of an aircrew a certain number of hours each week to support combat missions. His squadron's primary aircraft was the C7-A Caribou, a large transport bush plane manufactured by de Havilland Canada with Pratt & Whitney R-2000 radial engines. He also worked on AC-47s, which were C-47s—a military version of the venerable Douglas DC-3—converted to gun ships.

Dad's tour of duty ended in September 1970, and he married my mother in New York a few weeks later. Mom spent much of his deployment planning the wedding and praying for him to return home to her standing on his own two feet. The experience had a profound effect on each of their lives, as it did for so many others of their generation. I've only seen my father cry twice—once at the Vietnam Veterans Memorial in Washington, D.C., and once at his mother's funeral.

He never completed his degree in engineering after returning from Vietnam, but took classes in business administration at the local community college. It was there that he saw an advertisement for a private pilot ground school. After completing the ground school and passing his FAA written test, he decided to spend his veterans' benefits on flying lessons, a decision for which I am forever grateful. He went on to earn his private and commercial pilot certificates as well as his instrument and multi-engine ratings.

When I was a baby he worked for an engineering management company whose clients were the regional power companies, climbing the high-tension electrical towers that he would later learn to avoid while flying airplanes. Then, when I was in elementary school, Dad's entrepreneurial spirit got the best of him and he started his own business selling and installing home security systems. He was president of the local and state alarm associations for many years, and used his flying skills to attend regional board meetings all throughout New York state. He ran his business as a small company for more than 20 years, employing several people whom he treated like family. His attention to detail and focus on providing excellent customer service made a lasting impression on me, and I've tried my best to emulate that approach in my own flight instruction business.

I admire my father for being a determined survivor of all the struggles he's faced in his life. On the dashboard of his beat-up old Jeep he keeps a simple note to himself that reads: NEVER GIVE UP.

***

Two weeks after we returned from our Thanksgiving trip, I was looking at the calendar and, as I did every month, wondered whether Dana and I might have gotten lucky in New York. The days passed without any of my usual premenstrual symptoms, and overall I just felt a bit different. After an otherwise uneventful day of teaching that Friday, I awoke in the middle of the night with mild cramps and expected to find spots of blood, but there wasn't even a trace. I grabbed a pregnancy test stick from the pantry and decided to confirm what I already thought I knew, that my period would arrive the next day. I sat there sleepy eyed, watching the blue tint travel through the first window into the second window of the test stick.

But then I noticed something odd. There was a blue line forming in the first window. I could not believe what I was seeing. I waited a few more minutes and the line grew darker. Two blue lines equals pregnant. I was pregnant.

I ran upstairs and jumped back into bed and woke Dana. "What?" he said. "Guess," I said, giggling. "You're pregnant!" It was still dark but I could see the smile on his face. We laughed and held each other until the sun came up.

It was a surreal feeling, knowing that somewhere inside me a little person was forming. My child. Our child. I never thought I'd have the chance to experience being pregnant and being a mom. I thought about the first time I saw Dana hold that little girl at the company party and how that sparked something in me.

It still didn't feel real, though. The next morning I confirmed the first result by repeating the test using another brand of strips. I asked Dana if he thought I should keep my scheduled flight lessons that day. We agreed that as long as I was feeling all right, which I was, I should fly. Still, I was hyper-attuned to what was going on inside my body, wondering if the little cramps I felt were a sign of something wrong, or just the little embryo making itself at home in my uterus. I'd read a lot of pregnancy blogs and online message boards, and learned many women experience some mild cramping and even light spotting in early pregnancy, so I dismissed it and went to work.

The standard 40 weeks of a pregnancy includes the first two weeks between your last menstrual cycle start date and conception. I'd been using ovulation prediction kits to target the optimal date for us to conceive, and in November those dates just happened to fall during Thanksgiving weekend. So that meant that our little baby was probably conceived in New York, near the place where I was born and raised, where I've always felt at home.

Just a few weeks before Thanksgiving, I'd visited my gynecologist for some advice on how to get pregnant faster. Some of my female friends who got pregnant in their late thirties and early forties had suggested I start taking a drug to facilitate ovulation, but I wanted an expert opinion first. My doctor just looked at me and smiled. "You know, you are young. So young, and healthy," she said. "You and your husband just need to go on a vacation and relax, and it will happen." I liked her attitude and left the meeting feeling more confident in my body, and in nature's ability to do its thing.

After I learned I was pregnant, Dana and I immediately began talking about our trip in the Cub and what impact the pregnancy would have on our plans over the next year. My health insurance included a maternity rider, so I was covered for all prenatal care and delivery. We originally planned to start the trip in June, which meant I'd be about six months along when we left home, and we'd be in Oshkosh less than a month before my due date.

Some doctors discourage women from traveling on airliners during the third trimester, let alone in a small airplane. But maybe I'd be feeling great, with no complications. Maybe I wouldn't get so huge that my belly would get in the way of the control stick. Maybe I'd have one of those storybook pregnancies where I'd eat whatever I wanted, never get sick and have so much energy that I'd walk myself to the hospital, arriving exactly 10 minutes before the baby. Just days before I found out I was pregnant, Dana and I were discussing the weight limitations of the Cub and joked that if I was pregnant during the trip, he'd need to lose 15 pounds to compensate for my weight gain and still have enough room left over for our camping gear.

I decided that I was going on that trip, no matter what. Why should being pregnant prevent me from flying a small airplane around the country? Dana would be with me the entire time, and our flight legs would be very short by design. Our Cub only carried enough fuel to fly for about three hours at a stretch (with a one-hour reserve) and we'd planned to stop every hour or two anyway, for comfort. The only major change I could see us making to the plan would be leaving a few weeks earlier, which would mean missing Oshkosh. We would just have to see how I was feeling in the spring.

One of our inspirations for deciding to do this trip was Pat Moon, a former student and good friend of Dana's. Pat was diagnosed with non-Hodgkin's lymphoma in February 2009, but instead of curling up in a ball on the couch to contemplate his own mortality, Pat decided to run the Iditarod dog sled race through Alaska the following year. Certainly if Pat could tackle that physically grueling adventure in the dead of winter while recovering from cancer, I could cruise leisurely around the lower 48 in a Cub during the summertime while carrying a baby inside me.

When I called my parents to tell them I was pregnant, my mom squealed into the phone. I envisioned the huge smiles on their faces and wished I could be there to hug them. My parents have endured some pretty rough times, financially and emotionally, during their marriage and it made me feel great to be able to deliver a bit of happiness. They probably had given up hope of ever becoming grandparents, since I'm their only child. I regretted spilling my pain into their laps over the years. I knew it was incredibly difficult for them to see me unhappy for so long, and their stress level was, in part, linked to mine. I hoped my new life with Dana brought them peace of mind, and this baby would give them something to look forward to as they grow older.

I told only one non-family member about the pregnancy, my dear friend Bob Gawler, a flight instructor and the FAA-designated pilot examiner at our airport. Bob, a gentle, wise and patient grandfatherly figure and friend to me, was there for me during my darkest moments, when staying healthy enough to fly was a daily struggle. I've shared with him just about every painful detail of my life. When Bob saw how happy I was he gave me a huge hug and kiss on the head and started calling me "Mama" when he passed me in the hallway. I decided to otherwise keep my news under wraps until after my first sonogram, which was scheduled for January 9, 2012.

Dana and I spent the next few days getting accustomed to our new reality and began trying to develop a relationship with our new creation. He'd text me during the day and ask, "How are my babies?" We'd read that at about five weeks a baby is only the size of a poppy seed, so we started calling it Pop. I didn't really feel any different, except perhaps a bit more bloated than I otherwise would be before my period began. My jeans felt tight, and fearing squishing the baby, I put a rubber band through the button hole and wrapped it around the button to give myself a little more room. Other than that, I had not yet developed any of the common pregnancy symptoms such as nausea, fatigue or headaches.

On Friday, December 16, just five days after I found out I was pregnant, I went to the bathroom during my lunch break and discovered a light brownish stain. Within the hour, it had turned blood red. I texted my afternoon client and apologized for canceling at the last minute. There was no way I could fly with that on my mind. I went straight home and called my doctor's office, and was told by a nurse that as long as the bleeding and cramping were mild, less than a normal period, I shouldn't worry. The nurse said this is common as the baby is implanting itself into the uterus and closing up the hole so it can grow there for the next nine months. I was terrified, though, because it felt just like a period. I curled up on the couch, hoping it would go away but knowing that if it didn't, it meant our little seedling didn't want to stay, that something was wrong, and our brief moment of glory was coming to an end.

By the time Dana came home from work an hour later, the cramps had intensified and I felt as if my period had begun in full force. As soon as Dana walked in the door and I saw the concern on his face, I started wailing uncontrollably. I hadn't let out such intense, deep sobs in a very long time. He held me close until I calmed down enough to get up and go the bathroom and face the truth. The water in the basin was crimson and the urine test confirmed that my pregnancy was over before it really had a chance to begin: Just one blue line. I had miscarried. We snuggled on the sofa together and cried, allowing ourselves to process what had just happened, to let the emotions roll over us like a raging thunderstorm.

Even though we were both disappointed and sad, we trusted nature's infinite wisdom to guide our bodies to their intended destinations. All we could do was take care of one another, live a healthy life as best we could and enjoy each day to the fullest. With the exception of an occasional glass of beer or wine at a dinner out with friends, we had stopped drinking alcohol altogether. I'd switched to decaffeinated coffee, shopped for organic groceries and was taking prenatal vitamins every day. I felt I was doing everything right for once in my life, but still, my body let me down.

We went to sleep that night exhausted, but woke the next morning with renewed hope that nature might give us another chance. I felt even if I never got pregnant again, I could live peacefully with the knowledge that we succeeded, if only briefly.

Chapter 9
Bringing Home Baby

By the time Christmas arrived, Dana and I had put the miscarriage behind us and we enjoyed a relaxing weekend at his brother's house in North Carolina. Marc had called me a few days before we arrived to ask if I could bring Dana's radio-controlled airplane transmitter, but to keep it hidden. He had a surprise gift for Dana under the tree. When Dana tore the paper off of the huge box to reveal a miniature version of our Cub, we all broke out in laughter because Marc didn't yet know that we'd bought a real Cub when he ordered the gift.

With a forecast for mild temperatures and clear skies for the next several days, Dana and I boarded an airline flight from Baltimore to Orlando on Friday, December 30, 2011 to pick up our Cub. In our two small carry-on bags we'd packed a few changes of clothes, essential toiletries, navigation charts, a portable GPS and VHF transceiver, spare batteries, our headsets, my laptop and our iPhones. Barring any weather or mechanical delays, it would take us three casual days to fly about 800 miles from the private airfield in Florida where the Cub sat to its new home in Maryland.

The next morning the seller met us for breakfast at our hotel and drove us out to the residential airpark where he lived. Every home there includes a hangar that backs up to a meticulously maintained grass airstrip. A thick layer of fog hung over the entire Orlando area at dawn but the forecast called for it to lift by 11 a.m. That would give us enough time to inspect the airplane, review the maintenance logs and sign the necessary paperwork to make it our own.

The airplane was beautiful, neat and spotless. What was even more beautiful was the look of joy and pride on Dana's face as he inspected the airplane. Then, before I had completely absorbed the fact that we were owners of a Piper Cub, the sky had cleared and Dana was telling me to climb into the back seat and get ready to go. Our journey was about to begin.

Starting our Cub's four-cylinder, 90-horsepower engine required proficiency in the ancient art of hand-propping. Most modern airplanes, like cars, can be started from inside the cockpit by simply turning a key or pressing a button. Our Cub, however, was built before such systems were available in aircraft.

First, the pilot must prime the engine by drawing some fuel into the intake manifold. In a Cub this can be done using a manual primer located inside the cockpit or by pulling the propeller through a few times. The ignition system uses magnetos, which generate electricity for the spark plugs in each cylinder. But magnetos must be turning to generate that electricity, so some mechanical force has to be applied. In modern airplanes, that force is provided by a small electric motor called a starter, which gets the propeller turning and the magnetos spinning. But in our Cub, the mechanical force was provided by someone pulling the propeller through by hand. When the spark plugs fire, they trigger the combustion process that is converted into mechanical energy to spin the propeller. The engine will then continue to operate until it runs out of fuel or the magnetos are switched off.

In addition to inconvenience, the main disadvantage of hand-propping over an electric starter is that serious injury or death can occur if the person turning the propeller doesn't remain clear of the spinning blades. You have to get your hands and body away from the propeller immediately after pulling it through. Dana has a scar on his left wrist from when he dropped his guard while hand-propping a friend's plane and didn't get his arm out of the way in time. He was very lucky he didn't lose his hand, or worse. He showed me how we could start the Cub as a team, using specific actions, verbal commands, and responses. This would ensure our safety and help prevent any more injuries.

With bags packed and ready to fly, I strapped myself into the back seat of the Cub on that warm December morning and held the brakes tight. Dana said, "Switch off" and I confirmed that the ignition switch was in the OFF position. "Switch off," I replied. "Brakes," Dana said next. I held the brakes firm and replied, "Brakes set." Dana pushed on the propeller hub to confirm that the brakes were holding. I held the throttle in the full idle position as Dana turned the prop through a few times to prime the engine and when he was ready, he said the word that is probably most associated with hand-propping airplanes in old movies: "Contact!"

Pilots are taught to treat airplane propellers like loaded guns that can fire at any time, even when the ignition switch is turned off. By repeating the word "contact," I let Dana know I'd switched the ignition on and was ready for him to start the engine. Standing with one foot behind him, he put the palms of his hands on the right propeller blade (as viewed from the cockpit) and pulled down on it while shifting his body weight toward his back foot. It's a physical movement that reminds me of a pitcher winding up to release a baseball. By the time the engine fired, Dana had shifted his body safely away from the propeller and was ready to climb into the plane with me.

And I do mean climb. The interior of a Cub is extremely small, with scarcely more room than a two-person kayak. The front seat pad measured 12 inches square, while the comparatively luxurious rear seat was 12 inches deep by 24 inches wide. At 6 feet 2 inches tall and 190 pounds, Dana had to hoist his long legs into the cockpit while holding onto the steel framework above the instrument panel, being careful not to kick a hole in the fabric covered fuselage. Dana fit more comfortably in the rear seat, but on the first leg of our journey he sat in the front so I could get accustomed to the view from the back seat, where the pilot sits when flying solo. After our first fuel stop, I moved up front so Dana could stretch out a bit.

Even though I'm just 5 feet 5 inches tall and weighed 120 pounds, I still had to flex my frame quite a bit to get into the Cub without kicking it. It's sort of like doing a pull-up at the gym. I thought to myself, "If I'm pregnant during our trip this summer, I have no idea how I'm going to haul my fat belly into and out of this plane." But I figured if Dana could get in it, so could I, belly or no belly.

It wasn't long after we'd left the ground that I fell in love with the newest member of our family. We cruised with the door and windows wide open, enjoying the warm Florida sunshine and the gentle, earthy scents rising from the marshes and farms 500 feet below. The GPS helped us weave around some restricted airspace, but mostly we navigated using paper charts and a compass, just as the first pilot who flew this plane would have done in 1938.

In today's technology-obsessed, information-addicted culture, it's often difficult to unplug for a few hours to relax and enjoy life's simple pleasures. Like many Americans, I spend a lot of time on the computer. I use social media primarily as a business tool, so during the first few hours of the flight I found myself constantly checking my phone for messages, and even posted a few updates from the air while Dana was flying. FAA rules prohibiting the use of portable electronic devices on airline flights didn't apply to us flying in the Cub. We didn't have any critical navigation equipment that could be threatened by an errant cellular signal, although the magnetic compass deviated by a few degrees if I held the phone close to it. Cell phones work well from the cockpit of a small plane flying low, though text messages are more practical than voice calls due to the engine noise.

After a while I realized that nobody needed to know exactly what I was doing in flight at every moment. The whole point of the adventure was for us to enjoy ourselves, explore new ground and learn from the experience. Tweets and blog entries could wait until after the plane was safely tied down at the end of the day. After the second fuel stop I turned the phone off, restarting it just before landing to check the surface wind speed and direction using a specialized aviation application.

We decided the flight home from Florida would count toward our 48-state goal, since we'd land in six states along the way: Florida, Georgia, South Carolina, North Carolina, Virginia and Maryland. After a fuel and lunch stop in Fernandina Beach, Florida, we continued north with the goal of making it to Myrtle Beach, South Carolina, by sunset. Our Cub didn't have a battery or any onboard source of electrical power for lights, which meant we couldn't fly it after sunset. As we cruised up the Atlantic coast over long stretches of deserted beaches, without a human settlement or airport for many miles around, Dana and I realized that we were about to leave the state of Georgia without having landed there. And so it was that only a few gulls fishing off the shore of Ossabaw Island noticed as Dana and I slowly descended, touched the left wheel briefly on the sand, and then flew away.

By the time the sun set on 2011, we had traveled about 220 miles, landing in Beaufort, South Carolina, a few miles inland from Myrtle Beach. While many of our friends were partying and toasting the new year at midnight, we were fast asleep in our hotel room, dreaming of what the next day—and the new year—would have in store.

We called a taxi service before we went to bed to make sure a driver would be available to pick us up at the hotel at 6:30 a.m. to drive us to the airport. We were shocked when the driver arrived on time, but he confessed that he'd been up all night and we were his last fare. The taxi reeked of cigarette smoke but the driver was remarkably pleasant, considering he'd probably endured a long, grueling night. When we pulled up to the airport there were two police cars in the parking lot, with lights on and engines running. Apparently the Beaufort airport is home to a local police outpost. I was relieved that our Cub had been secure overnight, since we had forgotten to bring an anti-theft lock for the propeller.

It was amazing to watch the sun rise on New Year's Day at an airport with our airplane, just the three of us and the purple sky. I thought about how two short years ago I'd greeted the new year alone with a pounding headache. This was a considerable improvement. My life had completely turned around since I'd met and married Dana, and we were just getting warmed up.

We took off shortly after 7 a.m. and headed for Kitty Hawk, North Carolina, the place where brothers Wilbur and Orville Wright became the first humans to achieve powered flight on December 17, 1903. It's incredible to think that just 34 years after that precarious first flight, the first Cub was delivered, making personal air travel accessible to everyday people and marking the beginning of a movement we now know as general aviation. I give a lot of credit to Dana's friend, Mark, and his partners for bringing Dana to Washington, D.C., to work for Matchbox, because if Dana had stayed in Chicago we likely never would have met, except perhaps by chance, as strangers at an air show. But I also owe a big thank you to those two bicycle makers from Ohio for following their dream. Without the Wright brothers' passion and courage, who knows if Dana and I would have had the privilege of flying a small airplane around the country to follow our own dream.

After a short visit at Kitty Hawk, we took off and headed north toward Norfolk, Virginia, where we would put down for the night. Dana's mother, Betty, lives in a retirement community in nearby Virginia Beach and was waiting for us at Chesapeake Regional Airport. She brought along two of her closest friends, who were very excited to see the plane. They were all just kids when the Cub was in its prime during and immediately following World War II, and seemed to connect in some way with its history.

I learned quite a bit about cross country flying in the Cub on the second day of our trip. First, whenever you're flying low, it's critical to have a place to land in case the engine quits. This concept was not new to me as an experienced pilot and flight instructor, but I'd never really contemplated flying hundreds or thousands of miles at an altitude I'd typically use for a short local flight. The straight-line course between fuel stops in Florida and South Carolina would have taken us over some wide areas of unpopulated marshland, so instead we followed roads and tried to stay over solid ground or beach whenever possible. When we had to cross a lake, river, or bay we maneuvered to stay over the narrowest stretch of it and climbed high enough so we could reach the shoreline without engine power. Also, it's important to watch for radio antennas, keeping in mind that most of the large towers, some of which are more than 1,000 feet tall, have wires that fan out from the top of the tower to the ground. They are all charted, but not always easy to see from a distance because they are so thin.

Our Cub's instrument panel was very simple, and only two of the instruments were really critical, anyway: the oil pressure and oil temperature gauges. The other two, the tachometer and altimeter, were marginally useful. The tachometer needle bounced around so much that we couldn't tell with any degree of accuracy at what speed the prop was spinning at any given moment. Instead we controlled engine power by throttle position and sound. The altimeter couldn't be reset in flight because it lacked an indication of barometric pressure, so we had to set it to the airport elevation on the ground before takeoff, and hope the barometric pressure didn't vary dramatically during the flight. This was rarely a problem since we only traveled about 200 miles at a time, at low altitudes that were easy for us to judge accurately just by sight—generally about 1,000 feet above the ground, sometimes a little more, sometimes a little less. I checked the altimeter against the altitude shown by my iPhone's GPS at various points during the trip from Florida to Maryland, and it was always accurate within 100 feet.

Our Cub didn't have a fuel gauge like most airplanes. The way we knew how much fuel was left in the main 12-gallon tank was by observing the behavior of a little red steel rod which I named Fred the Fuel Dude. Fred was a funny little guy because he was attached to a cork that floated and bobbed around on the fuel in the tank, so in flight it appeared as if Fred was constantly doing a little dance, like a hula doll on the dashboard of a car. When Fred's head (the bent part of the top of the rod) dropped down and nearly touched the top of the fuel cap, the tank was almost empty and it was time to either transfer fuel from the 12-gallon auxiliary wing tank into the main tank, or land and fill up. The Cub's fuel endurance far exceeded our own, however, so when Fred said he was hungry, our sore rear ends were already telling us it was time for a break.

You can never be in a hurry when traveling in any light airplane, especially an old, slow one like the Cub. I've somewhat jokingly used the analogy that flying across the county in the Cub wasn't much different than driving a car, except there were no speed traps or tolls to worry about. There are, of course, many more considerations when flying long distance than there are when driving, mainly the weather. Our overnight stop with Dana's mom in Virginia Beach was strategic because we knew, based on the forecast for Monday, there was a chance we might not be able to complete the flight to Fallston due to strong winds. If we had to spend an extra night anywhere and wait for calmer conditions, we wanted to spend it with family.

When we woke up on Monday morning, the forecast still called for gusting northwesterly winds at the surface throughout the Mid-Atlantic region. Since we flew so low most of the time, the winds aloft forecast (for flights 3,000 feet above the ground and higher) was largely irrelevant to us, but could help us anticipate turbulence. When the winds at 3,000 feet are forecast to be 30 knots or greater, you can generally expect some turbulence. The sky was mostly clear, but experience told us the ride might be a bit rough. After considering all the available information, we decided it was safe enough to fly, but we needed to decide where we'd go if we were unable to land at Fallston.

The runway at Fallston is oriented from southwest to northeast and, with surface winds forecast to be out of the northwest, we would be dealing with a strong, direct crosswind during the landing. The Cub, when flown by an experienced pilot like Dana, can be safely landed in a 15 to 20-knot crosswind. Dana said he'd attempt the landing at Fallston and, if he was unable to handle the crosswind, we'd divert to nearby Harford County Airport, where the crosswind component would be more manageable. I called ahead to Harford and arranged for a taxi to be available to take us from there to Fallston, where we'd left one of our cars. The other car was parked at Baltimore-Washington International Airport, where we'd caught our flight to Orlando.

The flight from Chesapeake Regional Airport north along the west shore of the James River was gorgeous, with only light turbulence at 500 feet above the ground. It was sunny but very cold, and we were glad we had packed layers of warm clothes to wear during the last segment of the trip. We flew over the Holladay family farm in Carrollton, Virginia, where Dana spent many summers as a child, and rocked our wings at his former babysitter, who lives nearby and was standing in her yard waiting for us. As we continued north past Williamsburg, crossing the York and Rappahannock Rivers, familiar landmarks along the Potomac River began to come into view. Our last fuel and rest stop was St. Mary's Regional Airport, located a few miles south of the Special Flight Rules Area (SFRA), the restricted airspace around Washington, D.C. To get from St. Mary's to Fallston, we'd have to remain outside the SFRA since the Cub did not have the required equipment, a transponder, which is a device that sends and receives radio signals that uniquely identify an aircraft on an air traffic controller's radar screen. Without this device, the Cub would appear on radar as a slow-moving unidentified target and be subject to military interception.

I felt a bit anxious flying close to the SFRA without a transponder, even though I knew we were perfectly legal. I turned on our handheld radio and used it to contact the control tower at Martin State Airport, which is located just outside the SFRA and a few miles southeast of Fallston. When I requested permission to fly through their airspace, the controller asked me to "squawk ident" which meant activating the transponder so he could observe us on radar. My heart jumped as I replied, "Cub 1938C, negative transponder." The controller simply acknowledged and cleared us through his airspace.

I'd spent the last 10 years flying near Washington, D.C., where pilots of small airplanes are treated by the government as potential terrorists first and law abiding citizens second. I realized how much I appreciated the freedom and serenity of flying the Cub low and slow over the countryside and couldn't wait to get it, and us, away from Washington. But at that moment, I was eager to get the plane on the ground at Fallston.

After nearly 14 hours of flying since we'd left Florida, we finally had Fallston in sight. The air had become very rough by then, knocking the Cub around like a kite. I held the radio and charts tightly and got my big fat hiking boots away from the rudder pedals so I wouldn't interfere with Dana's landing. He did most of the landings during that trip because I wasn't able to feel the pedals properly while wearing those boots. I traded utility for comfort, and decided if I was going to learn to fly the Cub like a pro, I needed to wear smaller, softer shoes.

Dana descended into the traffic pattern and flew low over the runway once without touching down to get a feel for what the wind was doing close to the ground. While the wind was very strong just above the treetops, it calmed down dramatically within 100 feet of the runway. On his second pass, Dana carefully touched the front wheels on the ground and kept the tailwheel right where it should be, directly behind us, until the plane came to a stop in the grass by our new hangar.

It was a relief to both of us to get the plane shut down and secured after that rodeo ride, and we were proud of ourselves for exercising such good judgement and teamwork. We proved on that flight up the East Coast that we could fly all around the country in the Cub, and with a few minor adjustments to our packing strategy, do so rather comfortably.

Chapter 10

Learning to Fly All Over Again

Dana and I spent the spring of 2012 getting to know the newest member of our family, and planning our summer adventure. Since Fallston is about an hour and fifteen minute drive from our house in Rockville, we could generally only go there on weekends. From January through the middle of June we logged about 10 hours in the Cub, flying to local grass strips so I could learn how to take off and land this simple, yet humbling tailwheel airplane.

You'd think learning to fly a tailwheel airplane would be easy for an experienced pilot and flight instructor like me, but not quite so. The thing that makes tailwheel airplanes so difficult to master compared to tricycle gear airplanes is their inherent directional instability during takeoff and landing. Because the airplane's center of gravity is located aft of the main landing gear, they tend to act like weathervanes, with a natural tendency to pivot into the wind. The pilot has to maintain the ailerons, elevator and rudder in the proper position to keep the airplane aligned with the runway.

Dana spent about six hours teaching me how to control the Cub in all kinds of wind. At times I felt like I was trying his patience, but his exceptional teaching and flying skills kept both our airplane, and our relationship, safe during my training.

My first solo in the Cub was not as life changing as my first solo in the Cessna 152 a decade earlier, but it was still a very significant moment in my flying career. On Saturday, June 9, 2012, Dana and I flew the Cub to Spirit Airport, a grass strip just south of Wilmington, Delaware, where our friend Mike Macario has a maintenance shop. We took it there for a routine oil change and to have Mike give it a thorough inspection before we departed on our cross-country trip. Mike and Dana changed the oil, inspected the spark plugs, and found the Cub to be in excellent health. Before we left, Dana asked me if I wanted to take it around the patch a few times by myself.

There was no particular reason why I should do it, other than to say with pride that I had truly acted as pilot in command of one of the world's oldest and most respected airplanes. Dana signed my logbook with the endorsement that allowed me to act as pilot in command of a tailwheel airplane, and for an extra $100, the insurance company let me fly it solo. But flying it solo once didn't mean I was confident enough to take passengers or even go up by myself in much wind. Flying any airplane, especially a tailwheel airplane, requires regular practice to maintain proficiency. The more hours you have in a particular make and model, the easier it is to fly. But it still requires practice.

A month passed between my first Cub solo and my next flight in it with Dana—just enough time for me to develop some serious rust. My first few landings at Harford County Airport were fine, but then the wind shifted from the south to the west. I had a direct left crosswind on takeoff, which meant the Cub's nose wanted to turn to the left on takeoff even more than it normally does. The main control you have over the airplane's direction is the rudder, but the rudder needs air flowing over it for it to be effective. Well, I raised the tail before I had gained enough speed and—bam, the nose veered sharply to the left almost instantly.

"Baby! Take it!" I screamed to Dana as I pulled the throttle back to idle to abort the takeoff. "I have it," he said calmly while pushing the right rudder pedal to the floor, adding full power, and continuing the departure. My mistake was getting the tail up too quickly.

"That was a result of gyroscopic precession, coupled with raising the tail too early with a fairly strong crosswind, Mer," Dana said as a he handed the controls back to me. "Next time, don't be in such a hurry to get the tailwheel up. Push the throttle in slowly and hold the tail down for a few seconds until you pick up more speed, then push forward on the stick to raise the tail while adding enough rudder to keep the plane aligned with the runway. You'll have much more control that way."

Once again, I learned a valuable lesson that not only would make me a better pilot, but would help me deal with other life challenges, too. Don't rush. Take my time. Stay in control. *Fly the airplane.*

Chapter 11
Off to Look for America

On Friday, June 29, Dana and I drove Booey up to New York to drop him off with my parents, who were eager to begin hosting doggie summer camp. It was tough leaving him, but our minds were focused on our mission and getting everything ready for our departure on July 1.

As we returned home later that evening, we noticed some lightning in the sky to the west. I checked the radar and saw a solid line of severe thunderstorms pushing east toward the Washington area. It was very hot that day and our upstairs bedroom felt like a furnace when we arrived, so we turned on the air conditioning and went to sleep in the spare bedroom downstairs, where it was much cooler. Within an hour the storms hit hard, with winds so intense that I was worried a tornado might be in the works. We don't have a basement in our house and I thought that if I heard the telltale freight train rumble, we'd head for the bathtub.

We woke up next morning sweating, because the power had gone out overnight, which meant no air conditioning. Trees and branches were down all over the place, and news reports indicated that it could be a week before power was restored to the more than one million people in the D.C. area who were in the dark. I called the Fallston airport manager to make sure the Cub was unharmed, and she said it was fine. What a relief. Dana and I joked to each other that if the plane had been destroyed by the storm, we'd make the trip anyway, in the minivan.

We got a hotel room near Fallston for the night because we wanted to ensure we'd get a comfortable, restful night's sleep before launching on our trip the next morning. Since we didn't have much room in the plane for clothes and supplies, packing didn't take very long. The laptop, paper charts, flip-flops and a spare quart of oil got tucked in the tiny baggage compartment, and a gym bag with our clothes, towels and toiletries sat on top of that. Our tent and sleeping pads were tucked under Dana's seat, and I kept a small sack with snacks, extra batteries and the handheld radio on the floor by my feet.

It was warm and sunny with good visibility when we departed Fallston at around 9 a.m. on July 1, 2012, heading northeast toward White Plains, New York, our first overnight stop. After touching down in Delaware and New Jersey, we followed the New Jersey Turnpike to Trenton, then turned right toward the Verrazano-Narrows Bridge at the mouth of the Hudson River.

Looking down at the turnpike reminded me of the first time I took a commercial airline flight from Washington to New York. I was in college, and back in those days you could buy a one-way airline ticket on the shuttle for about $50 with a student ID. It wasn't so cheap that I could afford to fly every time I wanted to go home, but on busy holiday weekends like Thanksgiving, when what normally was a four-hour drive could take up to eight hours, it was worth it. I remember sitting in that jet, feeling smug as I stared at the endless string of red tail lights creeping along the highway below. So as Dana and I flew over the turnpike in the Cub, barely passing the trucks that were lumbering through a construction zone, I felt a similar sense of satisfaction.

Simon and Garfunkel's "America" played in my head as I reached into my backpack for the handheld radio that would allow us to communicate with other pilots transiting the Hudson River corridor. There are always lots of sightseeing helicopters and airplanes over that narrow stretch of river, so the FAA encourages pilots to announce their position on a dedicated radio frequency. Dana flew while I concentrated on looking for traffic and announcing our position at the various recommended checkpoints: "Hudson Traffic, Piper Cub, VZ, northbound." I've flown this route many times before—past the Statue of Liberty, Central Park and the George Washington Bridge—and the thrill of it never fades. From about 1,000 feet above the river, you get to see Manhattan the way the pigeons and seagulls do. As a pilot and a proud American, it's also amazing to have witnessed the New York City skyline evolve since September 11, 2001. As we flew past the new World Trade Center buildings, which were still under construction at the time, I could not help but think about how that beautiful view of lower Manhattan was one of the last things many of the passengers on those two airliners saw before they died.

As we continued north past the George Washington Bridge, we could see the span of the Tappan Zee Bridge come into focus. At its western terminus is the quaint village of Nyack, with its grand old Victorian homes, art galleries, restaurants and colorful sailboats decorating the shoreline. Nyack is one of those unique small towns where mom and pop stores have survived for generations, where residents care deeply about their community, and where city dwellers escape for a relaxing weekend away from the frenzy of downtown Manhattan. I graduated from Nyack High School and absolutely loved growing up there, in the lower Hudson Valley.

The George Washington Bridge, New York City

After circling Nyack and taking some photos, we crossed the river and landed at Westchester County Airport, the same airport where my father learned to fly more than 30 years earlier. We parked the Cub at Panorama Flight Service, one of the companies (known as a *fixed-based operator* or *FBO*) at the airport providing fuel, parking and other services for the pilots and passengers of private airplanes. Panorama is a family-run business that prides itself on providing great customer service, and it shows. The owners have known my father for years and generously offered to provide us with free hangar space and fuel for the Cub. That donation saved us several hundred dollars and would be the first of many acts of kindness by friends and total strangers who helped make our trip both pleasant and economical.

After spending the Fourth of July holiday with friends and family in New York, we took off on July 5 and flew northeast into New England. It took us two days to get to Bar Harbor, Maine, with an overnight stop with friends just outside of Boston. The New England coastline was clean and natural looking, uncluttered by the crowded and tacky, but nostalgically lovable, boardwalk scene of southern New Jersey and the Delmarva Peninsula I've known my entire life. As we approached the Bar Harbor Airport, we flew over dozens of small islands, some of which were populated by just a few homes. Elegant sailboats cruised in between the islands, and I imagined living a peaceful existence in that place, catching our own lobsters for dinner and grilling them out on the dock next to our seaplane. Of all the places we visited that summer, the New England region was my favorite, though Dana says he most enjoyed the Rocky Mountains.

Bar Harbor was a great place to visit on a budget because the island offers free bus service subsidized by the National Park Service. We took the bus from the airport to our campground, and from there to Acadia National Park and downtown Bar Harbor. We spent two nights camping and our tent held up great, keeping us completely dry and comfortable during a thunderstorm the first night.

We woke up the next morning to beautiful weather for our visit to Acadia National Park. A friend had suggested we hike the Beehive Trail, so we went to the visitor's center and got a map to find the trailhead. The hike offers spectacular views of the park and appeared innocuous enough on paper, but if I'd read the fine print, which described it as "strenuous" and "very steep" with "iron rungs on ledges of exposed cliffs," I might have changed my mind. But the friendly park ranger who provided us with the map looked us over and pointed us on our way without hesitation.

Dana and I have gone on many challenging hikes together, and I'm comfortable with moderate rock climbing as long as it doesn't require the use of any special equipment to get up or down. We saw lots of people, including physically fit seniors and younger couples with children in tow, bounding down the hill as we approached the trailhead. I thought, how hard can this possibly be?

The first few hundred feet of the climb was on a rough but walkable path through beautiful forest, but slowly transitioned to a narrower footpath on a much steeper grade. Then the first iron rungs appeared. I looked straight up at the tiny dots of people slowly creeping up the cliffs above and said to Dana, "Are we really going up *there?*"

This marked a critical decision point: Do I continue up the hill with Dana, or head back down with my tail between my legs and wait for him at the visitor's center? I've always been terrified of heights, which surprises some people when I tell them I'm a pilot. I get vertigo when looking down from the tops of tall buildings and usually drive in the center lane when crossing a bridge. So how in the world was I going to get myself to the top of that mountain? When another group of teenagers and retirees passed us by on their way up, my decision was made: I had to continue.

That may have been the first time in my life I felt there was a real possibility I might die. Dana is much more physically coordinated than I am and is very sure on his feet, and I knew he wouldn't let me fall. Still, I was worried I would lose my grip on a rung and tumble backward, taking him down with me. It was a very steep incline with few natural features such as large bushes or low hanging tree branches to serve as safety nets. I didn't bring my hiking boots on the trip so I was wearing sneakers, which had decent traction but didn't provide much ankle support.

When we were about halfway to the top, I looked down at the path we'd just climbed and realized that continuing up to the summit was the lesser of two evils. I didn't see any possible way I could balance myself going back down without falling. Usually when I have to go down a steep, rocky hill during a hike, I'm able to sit down on the rocks and "crab walk" or sit and slide down. But that wasn't going to work there. We asked a few people who passed us along the way if the trail continued past the other side of the summit, and if so, was it less steep and strenuous than the way we were going up. They said the path on the other side was much longer but flatter, with a few lakes where you could take a rest. That would be my reward, if I could only make it to the top. All I had to do was keep moving forward, and not look down.

"*Fly the airplane*," I chanted to myself in between rapid breaths that I had to consciously control to avoid hyperventilating. "Don't look down. Just get to the next tree. Just get to the next rock. Baby steps."

I always feel more secure crawling over steep or rocky terrain, because keeping my center of gravity low reduces the risk that I'll lose my balance or fall. At many points on the Beehive, though, crawling was not an option. I had to stand up in order to reach the next rung and hoist myself up to the next step.

"Always have one hand on the rail or on a rock and you'll be fine," Dana reassured me. "I've got your back."

Dana said afterward that he wasn't scared during the hike, but he was intensely focused on where he was stepping and what he was doing, especially knowing what a hard time I was having. As we took a break under a tree near the summit, a woman in her thirties passed us on the path carrying a toddler on her back in a sling. She had thighs the size of large tree trunks and glided up the incline with the confidence of a mountain goat.

"Well, I feel like a real idiot for sitting here in a panic," I said to Dana with a nervous laugh. "Let's get this over with."

The last few hundred feet of the climb were brutal, but I was determined to finish it and not have our trip around the country end with me in a bloody pile at the bottom of the Bee-hive. I was so relieved when we got to the top and felt so proud of myself for not giving up. Of course, I managed to slip and sprain my ankle on the way down the other side, but it was a small price to pay for a huge personal victory.

Chapter 12
Friends and Inspiration

It was during our stay in the lush, picturesque foothills of Vermont's Green Mountains that we first realized our adventure would be defined not only by the places we saw and the things we did, but by the people we would meet along the way.

On July 9 we landed in Springfield, Vermont, for a visit with our friend Sandy Gilmour and his wife, Karen, at their home in nearby Woodstock. The Springfield airport manager, Larry Perry, is a friend of Sandy's who also runs a local hardware store. Larry offered to put us up for free in his hangar, and even bought us a tank of fuel. Larry's wife, Susan, runs a lovely bookstore with the help of their two adorable Bernese Mountain Dogs. Dana and I really enjoyed spending time with all of them and felt very much at home in Woodstock, probably because the town reminded us so much of Nyack.

Sandy, a fellow journalist, also introduced us to Paul Bousquet, a freelance writer. Paul is an aviation buff and Sandy thought he'd be interested in writing an article about our stop in Woodstock for the local paper. When we met Paul for lunch the next day, he was immediately drawn into our story. Not only did he publish an article about our trip, but invited us to stay with him and his wife when we got to Montana, where they have a second home. It was this chance encounter with Paul that set the stage for what would develop into a vast network of people who selflessly opened up their homes, businesses and lives to us as we made our way around the country. The friendships we made defined our journey and overshadowed anything else we did or saw during those two months.

Online social media played a huge role in growing this network. One of our Facebook friends, Bill Tracy, invited us to visit with him when we passed through the Cleveland, Ohio, area. Bill and his wife, Yvette, keep their Piper Super Cub hangared at a grass strip in Lagrange, about 25 miles southwest of Cleveland. Bill, who works the night shift as an airline mechanic, is a passionate and very experienced tailwheel pilot who has flown his Super Cub all over the country. When we told him we were thinking of visiting the nearby Lake Erie island of Put-In-Bay for lunch, he offered to fly over with us. We had a great time hanging out with Bill and got some amazing air-to-air photos of each other's airplanes.

Traveling almost daily, we quickly lost track of time as days and weeks seemed to run together in our minds. People would often ask, "So where were you two yesterday?" Sometimes we couldn't remember, and would have to stop and think for a few moments before responding, or check our notes to see where we'd spent the previous night. But before we knew it we were back in the Chicago area, landing at Dana's second home, Westosha Airport, on July 12.

Our plan was to spend about a week in the Chicago suburbs visiting with friends before heading to Oshkosh for the air show. Dana's former student, Rich Davis, and his wife, Jayne, put us up in their camping trailer that they had parked on their property a few miles from Westosha. They offered to have us stay in their house but thought we might prefer the privacy of the trailer, which we appreciated. They had other house guests that week, so it was nice to have our own space. Still, Rich and Jayne cooked dinner for us nearly every night and made us feel like part of their family, letting us borrow their spare car and take a relaxing dip in their hot tub.

They even got us free tickets to the Country Thunder music festival that was being held a few miles from their house. Dana and I appreciate all kinds of music, and I found myself drawn to the pop country I was hearing on the radio, not for its unabashedly Christian overtones but because many of the songs address everyday issues that reflect my own life experience: working hard to make ends meet, building and maintaining a family, personal courage, the fragility of life, falling in love, and the beauty of nature. One day I was driving to the airport and heard a song titled "Fly Over States" by Jason Aldean, one of the featured acts at Country Thunder. The song begins:

A couple guys in first class on a flight
From New York to Los Angeles

Kinda making small talk killin' time
Flirting with the flight attendants
Thirty thousand feet above, could be Oklahoma

Just a bunch of square cornfields and wheat farms
Man, it all looks the same
Miles and miles of back roads and highways
Connecting little towns with funny names
Who'd want to live down there, in the middle of nowhere

They've never drove through Indiana
Met the man who plowed that earth
Planted that seed, busted his ass for you and me
Or caught a harvest moon in Kansas
They'd understand why God made
Those fly over states ...

Those lyrics sent an emotional chill through me, because I realized that in just a few weeks, we'd be flying over those square cornfields and wheat farms, and stopping to refuel our Cub in dozens of little towns with funny names. That's why we were so excited when Rich and Jayne surprised us with the concert tickets and we learned that Aldean would be performing. When his band played the first few notes of the song, Dana and I got up out of our lawn chairs and hugged each other tight under the stars, in that plowed cornfield, our own midsummer, midwestern Woodstock.

During that wonderful reunion week, we got to spend lots of quality time with dear friends including fellow pilot Gary Puls, who has taken many lessons from Dana over the years. Gary keeps his airplane at Lake-In-The-Hills airport, where Dana learned to fly. Gary credits Dana with giving him the confidence and experience he needed to complete his private pilot certificate, and as a show of gratitude Gary and his wife, Susan, were two of our most generous sponsors, pledging $10 for each state we landed in, for a total of $480.

Some of the most interesting experiences we had during the trip were completely unplanned and unexpected. On July 19 we made a day trip to Dyersville, Iowa, to see the *Field of Dreams* movie site. After stopping about halfway to wait for some morning clouds and fog to lift (which, by the way, was our only weather delay the entire summer), we landed at the Dyersville airport. The airport manager, Dave Kramer, left a car for us to use to get to the movie site, which is about five miles from the airport, on the opposite side of town. The movie site was well maintained and had a few visitors, even though it was a cloudy day in the middle of the work week. We did the usual tourist thing and walked into the tall corn, just as the ball players did in the movie, but aside from that there wasn't much to do or see (the farm house is off limits to visitors), so we drove back through town to the airport.

Dave was waiting for us at the airport when we returned. We sat down in the hangar with him to have a cold "pop" (Midwestern slang for soda) and talk about our trip. I'm not sure why the subject came up, but Dana started telling Dave about a fellow Cub cross-country flier from California named Bern Heimos, whom we had called back in December to get some advice on how our Cub would perform in the mountains. It turned out that Dave has known Bern for years, because he often stops at Dyersville if his travels take him near that part of Iowa.

We thanked Dave for his hospitality, bought some fuel and took off toward Galena, Illinois, a quaint town just east of Dyersville where some scenes in *Field of Dreams* were filmed. With permission from the owner, who asked to remain anonymous, we landed at a private grass airstrip near Galena. He was nice enough to offer to drive us into town and pick us up when we were done sightseeing. As we pulled up to a stop sign on Main Street, our host stuck his head out the window and said hello to one of his friends, Mary Beth Forsberg, who was walking across the intersection wearing a black smock. She smiled and waved and told him to stop by later on.

We didn't pay much attention to this exchange until about half an hour later when we met Mary at Embe, the restaurant she owns with her son. It was mid-afternoon and the energy from our peanut butter and jelly sandwiches was already wearing thin, so we decided to stop at Embe for a snack. A chalkboard sign on the sidewalk advertised various dishes including cream of mushroom soup with artichoke and sun-dried tomatoes. Dana and I love good soup, so we decided to go in for a bowl. The restaurant was very quiet given the late afternoon hour, and we saw Mary behind the bar, attending to chores.

"That was hands down the most incredible soup we've ever tasted," Dana said to Mary with a smile as we walked up to the bar to shake her hand. He wasn't exaggerating; with perhaps the exception of the Maryland cream of crab soup we crave at home, Mary's cream of mushroom was the most perfectly textured and seasoned soup we've ever enjoyed. We explained that we were in the van driven by her friend who said hello to her on the street earlier, and that we had no idea who she was until we walked into the restaurant.

As we continued our conversation, we learned that Mary is not only a fabulous cook, but a budding children's book author. She showed us a copy of a book she wrote for her grandchildren about how to live within their means, and we couldn't help but smile. We told her about how we were working on a book ourselves, and felt an instant connection to this hard working, creative and talented entrepreneur.

"Let me fix you some sandwiches for the road," Mary said as we got up to leave. Dana offered to pay her for them, but Mary wouldn't have any part of it. She wagged her finger and said, "Oh, you won't be paying for anything here today!" She would only accept a big hug in return as we walked out clutching a large bag filled with two huge turkey subs, chips and pickles.

We thought about Mary and her business on the flight back to Westosha, and hoped that we would be able to succeed in our own way when we returned home. Even though we'd budgeted generously for the trip and were confident we could survive for several months on savings and flight instruction income, it was still a bit unnerving knowing that we were on our own, without even the shallow security of one full-time job between us.

Chapter 13
Anniversaries

On July 21 we left Westosha and flew 50 miles north to Hartford, Wisconsin, where the Cub Club, a formal group of Cub owners, was hosting a party for its members, their families and friends. We'd joined the club to make new friends, share experiences about Cub flying, and participate in some special activities that the club had planned around the type's 75th anniversary. The main event was a mass arrival of 75 J-3 Cubs at AirVenture on July 22. We had discussed at length whether or not we would participate in the mass arrival due to concerns about the potential for a mid-air collision with so many planes flying in close proximity. We decided we would participate but planned to remain extra vigilant during the flight, which would be relatively short, covering only about 40 miles. As it turned out, one pilot did lose sight of the plane he was following and flew right over it on short final to Oshkosh, missing it by just a few feet. It was a near disaster of which few people were aware.

On the day of the mass arrival, we started the engine a few minutes before 6 a.m. and departed about 30 seconds behind the Cub in front of us, climbing to 1,000 feet above the ground. The weather was perfect, with a clear sky and good visibility, which made it much easier to see the airplane we were following. The flight was uneventful and Dana made a smooth landing at Oshkosh. We had been selected by Brady Lane, an EAA writer, photographer, and videographer, to be one of three Cubs to be outfitted with video cameras to document the event, and were featured in a video that was posted to EAA's Web site later that week.

We parked in an area designated for vintage and classic aircraft camping, flanked by dozens of other Cubs. Fortunately we didn't have to camp during that hot week, because Charlie Garrett, the father of Mike Garrett, one of Dana's former students, let us stay in his luxury motor coach, which was parked adjacent to the ultralight landing strip. We had the air-conditioned bus all to ourselves and felt like undeserving celebrities, knowing that some of our friends were sweating it out in their tents.

The next morning was the second anniversary of Dana's marriage proposal to me on Compass Hill. It was also the day I expected my monthly feminine visitor to arrive. I didn't have any pregnancy tests with me, and rather than going to the store to buy one, I decided to just wait until the end of the week and see what happened. We walked up the hill and quietly appreciated how lucky we were to be there together, in that special place that will always mean so much to us.

The week flew by in typical Oshkosh fashion, with Dana running around all over the place to catch up with friends he hadn't seen since the year before. Dana had also just started working as a sales representative for Fleming Aviation, the Mid-Atlantic dealer for CubCrafters, a company that manufactures a modern, much-improved version of the venerable bush plane, the Piper Super Cub. While Dana worked at the CubCrafters booth for a few hours each day, I had time to sit in the cool quiet of our campsite, write and wonder whether I was pregnant. I felt a lot more normal than I did when I had the miscarriage back in December, so I decided to avoid caffeine and alcohol during the show, just in case.

On Tuesday morning we gave a presentation about our trip at the EAA Museum. About 50 people showed up, including some of our friends. I've always been terrified of public speaking, but having Dana there to share the load made it easy, comfortable and fun. We didn't have a script or fancy presentation, just a slide show of pictures that we'd taken up to that point. People seemed to be connecting in a very personal way with us and our story. The positive response to our project was actually a bit overwhelming. Throughout the trip we received dozens of calls and emails from people all over the country, telling us how they'd always wanted to take a trip like this but never had the chance or never found a way to make it happen. Some said they were following our progress on the Web so they could live vicariously through our experience. A few called or wrote to tell us about when they flew or drove coast-to-coast with a loved one years before, and how our story brought back fond memories of their special adventure.

The most poignant moments of our trip, though, occurred with people we've known for years. On the morning we left Oshkosh, Dana and I met up with a longtime friend of Dana's, who was volunteering at the show that day.

"Have you lost weight? You look like a million bucks," Dana said cheerfully to the woman, who we knew was rather thin to begin with.

"Yes, I have," she replied with a forced smile. "It's called the terminal cancer plan."

Our hearts and faces sank as she told us that cancer had spread throughout her body, and that her doctors had told her there wasn't much more they could do for her. She also said she didn't know how much longer she had to live, but she wakes up every morning, works through the pain and tries to do something positive with each day. We watched her walk briskly through the crowd, but we could tell when she finally sat down to take a break, she was exhausted and hurting. Before we left, Dana gave her a loving hug, knowing it could be the last time he'd get to see her. He put on his sunglasses and softly cried as we walked away toward the Cub.

As we departed Oshkosh and headed west to begin the next segment of our adventure, I couldn't help but think of the encounter with our sick friend that day, and how lucky we were to be physically able to do what we were doing. I thought about our future and how it would be just too amazing if I were pregnant. My body showed no outward signs of anything in particular going on, though I felt an odd tightness in my belly. I was anxious to go to the drug store to get a pregnancy test when we landed in Eau Claire, Wisconsin, for the night. After checking into our hotel we stopped for dinner, and on our way out of the restaurant I discovered a small bit of evidence that led me to believe my body had probably duped me yet again. I decided to skip the drug store, and we returned to the hotel feeling a bit let down.

Early the next morning we continued west toward Wahpeton, North Dakota. During our lunch stop in Alexandria, Minnesota, with no further evidence observed, curiosity got the best of me and I bought a few tests. When we returned to the airport, we ran into a pilot who was giving airplane rides to the children in his church. I looked at the kids and wondered. While Dana was talking to the pilot, I went inside to take a test.

And there it was. A plus sign. Positive. Pregnant! The evidence I found the night before meant our tiny creation was making itself comfortable inside of me. I walked out of the bathroom with the test in my purse, ready to show Dana. Just as I was about to open the door, my phone rang. It was Rusty Neal, one of my students, calling to say he had just passed his private pilot check ride. He was so happy he was on the verge of tears. I turned off all of my emotions about the pregnancy test result and allowed myself to direct my happy energy toward Rusty, who had worked so hard to achieve his goal.

Besides, I wasn't quite ready to accept the result as the truth. What if it was wrong? What if my body was playing tricks on me? I stood there talking to Rusty in a weird state of incredible joy for him, but quasi-disbelief of my own good news. I honestly didn't know quite what to think or feel at that moment. Part of me didn't want to get too excited, knowing I could lose the pregnancy at any time.

After I hung up with Rusty, I collected my thoughts, took another look at the plastic stick, and went outside to show it to Dana.

"We got a plus sign," I said quietly, with a smile.

"I told you that you were going to get pregnant on this trip," he said, lifting me up in a warm embrace. The reveal was considerably less dramatic than it was back in December, and I think we both felt a bit more reserved and cautious this time.

"It's just one test," I said. "Let's keep flying and see what happens."

I quickly became aware of physical changes that were going on inside my newly pregnant body, even though it was still too early for anyone, including me, to notice much change on the outside. I began to develop a heightened and rather warped sense of smell, which would prove to be the most bothersome and challenging symptom during my first trimester. Certain earthy scents that once were pleasing to me suddenly became violently repulsive: pine, sage, rosemary, dried flowers and wood smoke, to be specific. And it could not have happened at a worse time, as we prepared to cross the high desert plains and the Rocky Mountains, surrounded by sage brush, pine trees and acrid smoke from the numerous forest fires burning all over the western half of the country that summer.

Chapter 14
Survival of the Fittest

The Dakotas provided our first glimpse of true American wilderness, as we flew for hours over nothing but dry grass plains occasionally interrupted by a skinny dirt road stretching to the horizon. It was hard to imagine how anyone could survive in that desolate, harsh environment, yet clearly a few rugged individuals there were eking out a living. Though we didn't see many signs of human life, someone had to be looking after the hundreds of cattle we saw grazing in the blazing sun or cooling off at a watering hole. We wondered how the animals navigated between home and pasture, because their tracks seemed to lead nowhere. Sometimes as we'd pass over a herd, one or two would raise their heads to the sky, perhaps startled by the noise of our engine as it cut through the silence and the wind. Most of the animals ignored us, though, and just continued chewing.

We arrived in Sturgis, South Dakota on July 29, after flying over the Badlands and Mt. Rushmore, to find Sturgis busily preparing for its annual week-long motorcycle rally. The rally draws tens of thousands of motorcycle riders and enthusiasts each year, and wasn't scheduled to kick off for a few more days. With the exception of shop owners unloading trucks full of t-shirts, souvenirs, and beer kegs, the downtown streets were rather empty.

Dana and I parked the filthy old car we'd borrowed from the airport in front of a tattoo parlor, and enjoyed a leisurely walk on what turned out to be a pleasantly warm and sunny afternoon.

When we returned to the car about an hour later, we discovered the door locks were broken, so we had to open the trunk, kick the back seat down and use an ice scraper to unlock the back door manually. All we could do was stand there and laugh about it, because there was no charge for use of the car.

We didn't spend a dime on rental cars during the entire trip, and that was largely a function of the culture of general aviation. Many airports offer free loaner cars (called *courtesy cars*) for pilots to use, usually just for an hour or two, but occasionally overnight so you can get to and from your hotel more easily. The quality and age of courtesy cars varies dramatically, but more often than not, rural airports have older cars and airports near larger cities offer newer cars. For example, at a small airport about 30 miles outside of Billings, Montana, we borrowed a land-yacht station wagon with wood paneling on the sides that had a major engine issue. It kicked and bucked like a wild bronco and did not seem to want to shift out of second gear. We laughed at the thought of having to leave it dead on the side of the road somewhere between the airport and the diner we were looking for. It was maintained by a group of volunteers using donations collected in a coffee can at the airport. Donations must have been lacking in recent months.

Another way we saved money during our trip was by sleeping at airports instead of hotels, when suitable facilities were available. That same small airport in Montana with the land yacht courtesy car also offered a clean, comfortably furnished cottage for pilots to spend the night, complete with two full-sized sofas, a restroom with a shower and a refrigerator stocked with soft drinks. We slept like rocks and left a generous tip in the can.

Despite getting a good night's sleep in the cottage, I woke up the next morning, on July 31, feeling a bit fatigued and nauseated. We showered, packed up our things and drove to the only diner in town for breakfast, and for the first time ever, I couldn't drink my beloved morning coffee. It smelled all right to me at first, but after just one sip I had to push the mug away. Dana and I looked at each other and immediately knew what that meant. I called the waitress and ordered a cup of hot mint tea instead, and it tasted wonderful. Ginger tea was tolerable for a few days, too, but then the aroma of both mint and ginger made me want to vomit. I felt like I was in a constant battle with my environment and there was little I could do about it except try new flavors and limit my time outdoors.

Every day, after we were finished flying, Dana and I would walk or drive around town in search of grocery or drug stores that sold flavored candies and teas, or even scented lotions or small bottles of cheap perfume—anything that might soothe my senses. The only thing that seemed to provide me with limited enjoyment and relief was watermelon or strawberry flavored hard candy, so we stocked up on those and I sucked on them pretty much all day long.

On August 1, we landed in Townsend, Montana, to visit with Mike Ferguson and his wife, Jeanne. Mike is the local representative for the Aircraft Owners and Pilots Association (AOPA) Airport Support Network. We met Mike while planning our trip, at the suggestion of one of our friends who works at AOPA. The network was established so local volunteers can keep an eye on issues that might adversely affect their respective airports, particularly things like noise complaints or attempts to restrict airport operations or close them altogether. I serve as the ASN volunteer for our home airport, the Montgomery County Airpark in Gaithersburg, Maryland.

A couple of days before we landed in Townsend, Mike found out that his neighbor, Tracy Salmi, is an old friend of Dana's. This was a pleasant surprise, as Dana had last seen Tracy several years earlier when she was living in Hays, Kansas, and working for Rans Aircraft, one of the most successful small aircraft manufacturers in the world. Dana and I really liked the vibe of their small airpark community, where airplane hangars are built as part of the houses, just like automobile garages. Pilots can wake up in the morning and walk downstairs to their hangar, where their personal airplanes are waiting to take them on a beautiful sunrise flight.

This is exactly what we did the next day. Tracy's husband, Neil, who learned to fly in the mountains and is very experienced dealing with the local terrain, offered to lead us along the next leg of our trip, to West Yellowstone. Dana and I took off at dawn right behind Neil and Tracy, staying about a mile behind them. The plan was for us to follow the Missouri River south to Three Forks, then pick up the Madison River to Ennis, and from there, follow Highway 287 to Earthquake Lake and then Hebgen Lake, which leads to the West Yellowstone airport.

The route looked simple enough on paper, and we found Ennis easily. But once we passed Ennis, Dana and I realized that following the highway to the lakes was going to be a little trickier than it seemed. By the time we reached the bend in the road, the sun was blazing over the horizon to the east, the same direction we had to fly. As we squinted to follow the road as it bent through the mountain, we couldn't see the first lake, which was a critical visual checkpoint in that mountain pass. Were it not for my radio communications with Neil, who confirmed we were going the right way, we would not have made that turn blindly, not knowing whether we had chosen the correct pass.

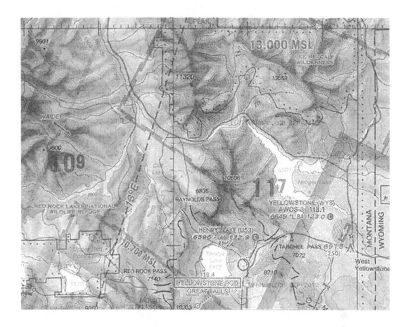

There were several passes going in that same general easterly direction, some with smaller roads that split off of the main road. They all looked pretty much the same to us, and we worried if we picked the wrong pass, we might get boxed in and not have enough room to turn around. Getting stuck inside a narrow pass is one of the main dangers of mountain flying, and we were grateful for Neil's expert guidance.

Once we got around the bend and saw the first lake, we were rewarded with a spectacular view, with green mountain ridges rising above us on either side and sparkling, clear water below. I secretly wished we had floats on the Cub so we could land on the lake and sail around for a while, enjoying the quiet serenity.

I snapped out of my floatplane daydream to hear Neil announce on the West Yellowstone airport frequency that we were inbound to land. The runway there is more than a mile and a half long, huge for our Cub but barely long enough for some jets considering the airport sits at an elevation of nearly 6,700 feet above sea level, where the air is thinner and airplanes need more space to take off and land. There were photos in the airport lobby of Air Force One, the presidential Boeing 747, landing there many years ago. That must have been an impressive sight.

After we tied the plane down and gathered our things, our journalist friend from Vermont, Paul Bousquet, arrived to take us all into town for breakfast. It was a perfect morning to sit outside and enjoy the cool air and warm sun, so we settled on a cafe with a large deck infused with the aroma of sizzling sausage and bacon, sweet waffles and coffee. My stomach was feeling pretty good that morning and I ate normally, but once again, I was only able to take a few sips of my coffee before abandoning it for hot tea. Something was definitely going on down there.

Neil and Tracy finished eating and said they should probably head back to the airport before it got too hot, which would make it harder for their airplane to climb into the mountains going back home. We said our goodbyes and spent the rest of the day driving around Yellowstone National Park with Paul. He took us to see the famous Old Faithful geyser and the numerous sulfur hot springs in the park. Oddly, the rotten egg smell of the sulfur hot springs didn't bother me as much as the pine trees, which along with brush-fire smoke would continue to plague me for the next 2,000 miles of our trip.

Paul was a warm and generous host, treating us as if we were his own grown children. The next morning we went on a short hike together to Ousel Falls, then drove a few miles north to a ski resort where we rode the chair lift up to Lone Peak at nearly 10,000 feet above sea level. I was a little nervous about getting motion sickness on the lift from the altitude and the dizzying view down the slope, but soon discovered I had nothing to worry about as long as I held onto Dana and the security bar.

"Fly the airplane, Meredith," I thought to myself as I took a deep breath of crisp mountain air and gazed down at the beautiful scenery below me.

Chapter 15
Signs of Life

We departed West Yellowstone on August 3, heading southwest toward the Snake River Valley in Idaho. Our goal was to arrive in Nampa, Idaho later that day to spend some time with our friends, Dorenna and Stace Schrader and their three grown children. Getting out of West Yellowstone was considerably easier than getting in, as we didn't have to fly through the same pass to get on course. Finding the valley proved easy and the first two legs were smooth, but by late morning the air had become very hot and turbulent. As we descended into the valley we got pounded by 30-knot headwinds, making our groundspeed less than 50 knots. I felt nauseated the rest of the day, and was totally exhausted by the time we arrived in Nampa at around 6 p.m.

The ever present dust and smoke in the valley was really starting to take its toll on my senses, and fuel fumes from the airplane gave me a sickening headache. Whenever Dana and I would stop to refuel, he was so careful not to spill any, but sometimes the pump wouldn't shut off when he wanted it to and fuel would pour out onto the cowling and seep into the cockpit beneath the front window trim. It would take about an hour for it to fully dissipate, which delayed our departure and made the day seem that much longer.

The bleak landscape in the valley wore on my mood and made me homesick. We flew hundreds of miles over barren acres of scrub brush and dried lava flows, broken only by the occasional oasis of a small pocket of irrigated farmland. When we started the trip, I was really looking forward to returning to the high desert paradise of Sedona for a romantic spa retreat with Dana, but in the heat of the Snake River valley all I could think about was how great it was going to be get to Atlanta and see my family. From there it would be a short, easy flight home through familiar territory.

I wondered if being pregnant was the source of my increasingly negative feelings and thoughts about traveling. Was my natural nesting instinct taking over? All I could think about was Booey and our family back home. I wanted to be near them all so badly it made my heart ache. As much as I was enjoying my hard-earned special time with Dana, I couldn't help longing for home.

I hated admitting it to myself and didn't want to share these thoughts with Dana at the time, but I also was starting to become somewhat disenchanted with the Cub. The novelty of flying low and slow around the country in a classic airplane was wearing off as I struggled to deal with the physical and emotional changes going on inside me. Every time we landed, I dreaded climbing back into the Cub to fly the next leg, even though I knew it would bring us that much closer to home. I was tired and cranky and sick of feeling sick all the time, and found myself fantasizing about finishing the trip in a faster, more comfortable airplane, like the Cessna 182 we flew on our wedding day. I even thought about abandoning the trip altogether and hopping on an airline flight to D.C. as soon as we reached San Francisco, just so I could at least say I managed to fly coast to coast.

"This trip is not nearly as important as your well being," Dana said to me one day during a lunch break when I felt so sick I started to cry. "If you really think you'd be better off at home, then let's get you an airline ticket. I can finish the trip alone. I'll be all right."

I knew he would be, but as soon as Dana reassured me with those words, I had a terrible series of thoughts. First, I imagined the Cub's engine quitting over hostile terrain, leaving Dana injured, alone and helpless somewhere in a mountain canyon or in the middle of the searing Mojave Desert. If that plane was going down, we were both going down in it together. I would not leave Dana alone to suffer.

Then my mind turned to our unborn child. What would he or she think of me years later if I failed to complete the mission, if I turned my back on my husband and our dream just because I was feeling a little sick? What kind of message would that send to the child about strength of character and resolve? And what about the hundreds of friends, family members and supporters who were cheering us on? What about the book? I decided I couldn't live with myself if I quit, and told Dana I wanted to press forward and finish the trip, but perhaps with a few modifications to the route that would get us home as quickly as possible.

A massive dust storm blew through the day before we left Nampa, covering everything, including the Cub, with a thick layer of acrid smelling dirt. Dana saw the storm approach as he was giving Dorenna a ride in the Cub. The rest of us watched from the ground as the miles-long, grayish-brown cloud slowly rolled over a nearby ridge line toward the runway. To me it looked like a giant thunderstorm, only silent and darker, without any lightning. I'd never seen anything so ominous looking.

By this time I'd lost sight of Dana and Dorenna, and started to get a little worried. Stace called his brother, who lives in a ranch up on the ridge, to make sure he was all right. He said he was fine, but that the dust cloud had reduced visibility on the ranch to less than a mile. There was no way Dana could fly the Cub in those conditions. I nervously stared up at the sky until finally, our yellow airplane rolled down the runway and parked in front of the terminal building right before the wind picked up. Dana said that he flew within about a half a mile of the storm to get a closer look at it, but it wasn't moving fast enough that he couldn't steer around it, even in the Cub. I guess it looked a lot worse from the ground than it did from the air.

As strange and foreboding as the high desert weather seemed to us, it couldn't douse the joy we felt seeing our old friends again. Signs of life emerged through the clouds of dust, giving me hope and boosting my nausea-soured mood. During our visit, the Schrader women and their girl friends were busy preparing for a bridal shower, to which I was spontaneously invited. Their home office was packed with gifts wrapped in shiny silver paper, bags of red silk roses, white candles and boxes of home-made candies for the wedding reception, reminding me of our living room in the days preceding our wedding at Davis Airport.

While I spent the afternoon with the girls, Dana hung out with Stace. I secretly wished that I was with the guys discussing aircraft maintenance instead of surrounded by giddy women at a bridal shower playing silly games, scrapbooking and talking about, well, other things, but I suppose it was good for me to take a break from flying and step outside of my comfort zone for a while. It was also kind of nice to be in an air-conditioned, dust-free house instead of an airplane hangar.

I've always been more of a tomboy than a girly-girl, preferring coed activities to those spiked with estrogen. As a child my favorite toys included construction sets and things I could build myself out of tape, glue, paper and cardboard boxes. I dabbled with makeup and big hair as a teenager in New York in the 1980s, but since then have adopted a simpler, more natural look. I occasionally wear dresses or skirts, but have always felt more comfortable, self assured, attractive and sexy in pants.

Only six percent of all U.S. pilots are women, and most of my female friends are also women pilots who seem to share my gender-neutral sensibilities. I opted out of a traditional bridal shower for each of my weddings, and was a bit uncomfortable when, during the party in Nampa, I was selected to be the model for my team's toilet-paper wedding dress. Despite my social un-ease with the popular game I went along for the ride and allowed myself to be wrapped in a roll of white paper while the bride-to-be took photos for her scrapbook.

I smiled with relief when she judged my team second place, and politely asked her to refrain from posting the photos on the

Internet. I knew it was all in good fun, though, and it made me happy to see this young woman enjoying her special day, her way. I thought about how when and if any of my friends or relatives offered to throw me a baby shower, I would probably choose to have a casual coed party at the airport, something that Dana could enjoy equally with me.

***

The Cub was coated in a thick layer of dust when we departed Nampa the next morning and headed northwest toward Seattle. Our intention was to arrive later that afternoon at a small airport located about 30 minutes northwest of downtown after a brief stop in Yakima, Washington. It would be a long day of flying, but the weather was good and we were well rested after a few days off. Dana and I each had a few friends to visit in the Seattle area, and since I'd never seen that city before, I was really looking forward to it.

Around lunchtime we landed in Yakima so we could tour the CubCrafters factory. The tour was fascinating but by the time we were ready to leave, I felt completely exhausted. Our choices were to spend the night at a hotel in Yakima, fly the remaining two hours to Seattle, or skip Seattle altogether and fly one hour south to Hood River, where our newlywed friends Michele and Tyler Sibley were expecting us the following day. Dana called Tyler to see if he and Michele would be home that night, and when he said yes, we decided to go there instead of Seattle. I was surprised at how easily my fatigue squashed my desire to visit a new city, but it was a quick decision at the time.

Our two-day stay in Hood River was an environmental relief for me, mainly because the air in the Columbia River gorge was clearer and smelled fresher, despite the pine under-tones. Hood River is a cute, young, outdoorsy town populated mostly by sandal-wearing kite-boarders. Nobody seemed to be in a hurry there. We hung out by the river and went out to dinner at a local brewpub, where I was conspicuously the only one who didn't order a beer. My stomach was bothering me a little bit and I thought the tea I requested might have given me away, but neither Tyler nor Michele said anything about it.

The next morning the nausea returned in force, and I called my gynecologist for advice on how to cope, and to make an appointment for my first prenatal visit on September 4, the week after we expected to return from our trip. She recommended I eat saltines and drink ginger tea, and said most women tend to feel better during the second trimester. I just had to tough it out for a few more weeks.

We left Hood River on August 9, toting tea bags, crackers and candy, following the Columbia River west to the Pacific. I wondered when I was going to feel better and be able to enjoy the trip as much as I did before AirVenture. I wanted so much to just relax and be a fun travel partner for Dana, but all I could think about was this little person forming inside me and the odd sen-sations I was beginning to feel, especially the nausea. I worried about whether sitting in the Cub for hours each day, breathing in brush fire smoke and fuel fumes, would be harmful to the baby. I had lost all interest in doing any of the flying, and for the re-mainder of the trip, settled into my job as copilot and navigator.

Dana was such a good sport throughout it all, and I hon-estly don't know what I would have done without him by my side. He was extra careful not to let any fuel spill out of the tanks when filling up, and we stopped more often so I could get out and stretch. If I was tired in the middle of the day, we'd land and take a nap together.

Despite skipping a few planned stops, the highlight of the western half of the United States for me was our brief visit in Florence, Oregon, where we first saw the Pacific Ocean. That's when we really felt like we had achieved something incredible, flying a small airplane from coast to coast. Seeing the beach lifted my spirits, and I couldn't wait for the salty air to fill my nose. It was cool and very windy at the airport, and Dana had a hard time getting the plane settled on the ground. After he landed we managed to secure the Cub in a parking spot with our ropes and drove the airport courtesy car into town for a few hours.

Florence is a small coastal village with lots of charm. It reminded me of Annapolis and some of our favorite small towns on Maryland's Eastern Shore, with an active marina, seafood restaurants by the water, candy and ice cream shops, galleries featuring works by local artists and, of course, tourists like us. We let our noses guide us down to the dock, where we found a young couple pulling live crabs from a crab pot and tossing them into a bucket of water. They were big and blue and tasty looking, and for a short while, I completely forgot about my nausea as I imagined sitting down to a heaping plate of them drowned in melted butter.

As we continued walking past rows of fishing boats, something in the water caught our attention. It was a small, gray spotted harbor seal swimming up to the dock to beg for food. We didn't have any morsels to offer the creature, but bent down anyway for a closer look. It raised its sweet looking face above the water for just a moment, wiggling its long whiskers and blinking its huge dark eyes at us, as if to say, "Hi there, got any food for little old me?" Realizing it had wasted its effort on us, it swiftly dove back under the dock and disappeared.

With just a few hours of daylight remaining, Dana and I drove back to the airport, carefully released the Cub from its moorings on the windy ramp and continued flying south along the beach toward San Francisco. Our goal was to spend the night at a romantic seaside bed and breakfast in northern California, but it soon became apparent we wouldn't be able to land anywhere within about five miles of the ocean due to a thick layer of clouds and fog. The layer stretched as far south as we could see. In fact, the forecast for San Francisco indicated even if we managed to get in somewhere along the coast, we could end up stuck there under the clouds for a day or more.

Granted, there are worse things in life than getting stuck with your husband in a lovely oceanfront town, but given how I was feeling, we both really wanted to keep moving. Besides, the Pacific coast was a lot colder than either of us had anticipated, so laying out on the beach in the sun or going for a swim in the shallows wasn't in the cards unless we flew much farther south, which we didn't have the time or energy for at that point. So, after heading a few miles south from Florence we diverted southeast and headed inland to spend the night at a nice hotel in Medford, Oregon. We still hoped to see San Francisco from the air in a day or two.

Chapter 16
California

Over the next three days we experienced some of the most dramatic climate changes we've ever encountered during a flight in a small airplane. California is a huge state containing a wide variety of ecosystems, terrain features and weather patterns. From Medford we flew south along Interstate 5 to Sonoma, California. On the way, we stopped in Weed for fuel and passed snow-capped Mount Shasta before encountering the lush, green hills of the Shasta National Forest. We had our sweatshirts on when we departed Weed, but as we exited the forest and continued south along I-5 past Redding into the Sacramento Valley, the air rapidly became hot.

The Cub's windshield turned the front seat into a greenhouse in the late morning sun, and I didn't get much cooling airflow sitting up there unless the window was open and I scooped it toward me with my hand. Dana was well-ventilated in the back seat, and also more shaded. I took the flight controls briefly while Dana removed his sweatshirt, then when he was flying, I removed mine and used an old chart to create a sun shade.

Our afternoon flight to Sonoma was brutally hot for both of us, and foreshadowed the conditions we'd be dealing with for the next week as we approached the Mojave Desert. But our overnight stop in the California wine country provided a tranquil reprieve from our airborne environment. We landed at Sonoma Skypark, a small, privately owned airfield flanked by some of the area's most famous vineyards. Sonoma is a charming town with quiet streets, perfectly manicured homes and gardens, and small, independently owned shops thriving on both local customers and tourists. We tied the plane down in the grass between the runway and a row of grape vines loaded with immature purple-blue fruit. Ron Price, the airport owner, met us there and invited us to stay with him and his wife, Donna, at their lovely home. We walked into town for dinner, returning the next morning to visit Ron's favorite bakery for warm croissants and coffee.

Later that afternoon we landed at Frazier Lake Airpark in Hollister, California. The airpark is located in a fertile area of the valley among fields of fragrant garlic and sugar beets, and features a unique water landing canal parallel to the grass runway. From the air it looked like a giant irrigation or drainage ditch, but after sweating our way through the valley, flying over mostly brown dirt fields, it was a pleasant surprise to arrive at Frazier Lake and discover that the grass strip was green and lush.

Monty Groves and his wife, Darcy, the pilot couple who manage the day-to-day operations at Frazier Lake, met us after we landed and offered to let us stay overnight in their hangar. They live about an hour away from the airpark and figured we'd prefer to stay in the hangar so we could get an early start in the morning, which we appreciated. Like most airplane hangars theirs was full of equipment and smelled of fuel, oil and dust, but it was quiet and—best of all—free. There was a comfortable sofa, a coffee maker and refrigerator in the hangar, and a clean, well stocked shower house with flush toilets on the property.

After we got settled, they drove us into town for lunch and stopped at Walmart so we could buy groceries and supplies. Later that evening, we joined them and a few of their hangar neighbors for a barbecue at the airport. Everyone there made us feel welcome, safe and cared for. But the best part of our visit happened just before midnight, out by the runway, as we sat bundled under a blanket to watch a meteor shower. Without any city lights to dilute our view, it was like being in a planetarium. The light show was spectacular.

"We really are lucky, aren't we?" I whispered to Dana as I snuggled closer to him to keep warm in the chilly night breeze. I had just taken a shower and washed my hair, which was still damp since I didn't have a blow dryer to use. We waited a few more minutes for another shooting star, then headed back to the hangar for the night. Dana slept on the floor on his sleeping pad, wearing his sweatshirt and covered with our sheet and warm blanket. I slept on the sofa, huddled inside Darcy's extra-warm sleeping bag. I don't know what I would have done without that sleeping bag, because it got very cold that night.

The next morning we departed at dawn and continued south along I-5 toward Bakersfield. We wore our sweatshirts and kept the windows closed to stay warm, as the temperature at the surface was only about 50 degrees. Normally, the air temperature drops as you gain altitude, but on this particular day we experienced the opposite effect, known as a temperature inversion. It got so hot in the cockpit that we had to immediately open the windows and remove our sweatshirts. The engine oil temperature was also rising, so we stayed low to avoid overheating. We also discovered that the air at around 500 feet above the ground was less bumpy than the air at our usual cruising altitude of 1,000 feet, so flying lower made our flight more comfortable.

Our first stop, Corcoran Airport, wasn't much of a break. Even though it was charted as having fuel available and there were no published notices to the contrary, we landed to find no evidence of a fuel tank, nor a single human being, anywhere on the property. The place was completely deserted except for a few junk-filled hangars and a couple of old crop dusters. It smelled weird to me, too. We had plenty of fuel to make it all the way to Bakersfield, but we were getting hungry and badly in need of a break. Whenever we approached an airport to land, we'd visually scope out the surrounding few blocks for signs of food and shelter in case we needed to spend some time there unexpectedly. But all we saw around Corcoran Airport were a few small houses and empty streets.

We piled back into the Cub and continued on to Bakersfield Municipal Airport, which advertised a restaurant right on the field. It was well over 90 degrees on the ground when we landed. The air conditioning in the terminal building was having a hard time keeping up with the heat, so our lunch break wasn't quite as refreshing and relaxing as we'd hoped. We shared a grilled chicken salad and a bowl of vanilla ice cream, and were back in the plane in less than an hour.

Our next stop, Tehachapi, was up in the hills and required a climb to 4,500 feet. We knew the Cub could do it, based on our experience climbing to over 6,000 feet on a hot afternoon near Rapid City, South Dakota. The Cub climbed slowly but steadily as we picked up Highway 58 eastbound toward Tehachapi. We passed over the Tehachapi Loop, built in the late 1800s by the Southern Pacific Railroad to allow heavy freight trains a shallower climb gradient going up the mountain and through the Tehachapi Pass. Airplanes sometimes perform a similar maneuver, climbing in a turn over lower terrain before crossing higher terrain. We didn't have to resort to such measures to get to Tehachapi, though we were glad to get on the ground and allow ourselves, and the Cub's engine, to cool off for a while.

The Cub may have benefited from the break more than we did, though. The air conditioner in the pilot's lounge shut down about an hour after we arrived, with outside temperatures by that time well over 100 degrees. It was late on a Sunday afternoon and it would be next to impossible to get anyone out there to fix it. We left messages with everyone on the airport's emergency contact list and got no replies. The thermostat was enclosed in a locked plastic case so it could only be adjusted by someone with the key, presumably the airport manager. Then Dana's ingenuity came to the rescue. He found a wire coat hangar in the bathroom closet and after shaping it a little, used it to poke inside the box to adjust the temperature. After a bit of fiddling with various settings, the unit kicked back on and wonderful cool air started blowing from the vents.

We stayed there until about 5 p.m., and a small passing thundershower did wonders to cool off the air and make the last leg of our day's flight more pleasant. Our next and final stop for the day was Lancaster, California, a suburb of Mojave. We were going there to meet Dana's former student, Sean Willis, who works as a design engineer at Scaled Composites, the company whose visionary founder, Burt Rutan, designed and developed the world's first private manned spacecraft, Space Ship One.

Sean had arranged for us to get a rare insider's tour of the Scaled Composites facility after we delivered a brown-bag lunch presentation on our project. About 50 employees attended our presentation, which was nearly identical to the one we gave during AirVenture. Everyone at Scaled was very laid back and genuinely interested in what we were doing, which to us seemed downright silly compared to building spaceships. Several of the employees came forward after our talk and told us that they too enjoy flying small airplanes, and wished they had more time to get up in the air.

The tour of the shop floor was absolutely amazing. We weren't allowed to take photos, but we were allowed to get up close and take a peek inside the latest and greatest Scaled design, Space Ship Two, which was built to carry civilians into space. We couldn't help but be filled with a sense of awe that we were witnessing history being created and that one day, we'd see that vehicle on television launching someone we know toward the stars. Maybe our child will get to ride in it one day. Maybe if we sell enough books we can buy a ride, too.

After the tour, we returned to Sean's house where his wife, Sara, was taking care of their infant son and preparing a wonderful smelling dinner of coconut jasmine rice and curried grilled pork chops. I got to hold the baby for a while and was so relieved that he didn't cry in my arms. I couldn't remember the last time I'd held a baby, and it felt surprisingly easy and natural. He made the cutest gurgling noises and seemed very relaxed and content. I hoped I could continue carrying our baby to term and have the chance to hold her that way.

Looking out through their kitchen window, I was abruptly yanked from my peaceful motherhood daydreams and drawn back into the reality of our flight across the desert. Sean and Sara's backyard was a microcosm of the dry, desolate landscape we would soon traverse in Nevada, Arizona, New Mexico, Utah and much of western Texas. Inside their house we were safe from the elements and surrounded by new life. But out in the yard, if you could really call it that, there was nothing but dust and rock, not a single blade of grass, not even a weed.

Dana and I contemplated going out for an after-dinner walk, but a quick step outside told my nose to stay indoors. The evening air was thick with the smell of a large brush fire that we'd observed in the hills earlier that day, instantly erasing the positive olfactory sensations I enjoyed during dinner. We took our showers and went to bed early, our thoughts returning to the Cub and our flight plan for the morning.

Chapter 17
Rough Terrain

The next two days of our trip were, from a flying perspective, the most challenging of the entire adventure, even more so than navigating the mountains. The desert southwest is vast and sparsely populated, and airports are spread farther apart than they are in other parts of the country. This meant we had to be extra careful when planning our route and our fuel stops. For safety reasons we opted to fly within gliding distance of major roads as much as possible, but there were places where we had to stray off course in order to see certain key landmarks like Monument Valley in Utah. Sometimes, flying direct from point A to point B was considerably faster than following the highway between those points, and we chose to go direct when we could remain over non-hostile terrain to minimize our time in the air and burn less fuel.

We departed Lancaster on August 14, with the goal of spending the night in Boulder City, Nevada, a medium-size town just east of Las Vegas. From there, we'd fly to St. George, Utah and then to Page, Arizona, which would be our staging point to view Monument Valley, an area of large sandstone buttes that lies within a Navajo reservation in Utah. One of Dana's former students, Brad Delisle, flies air tours out of Page and planned to meet us at the airport when we arrived.

The leg from St. George to Page took us over some rather rough terrain with few roads to follow and required a climb to 7,000 feet, but the morning was cool, clear and smooth, and the Cub climbed easily. We landed in Page around 10 a.m. and parked at Lake Powell Jet Center, one of two FBOs at the airport. The newly renovated building featured tinted glass floor-to-ceiling windows, plush leather couches and chairs, and an ample collection of complimentary treats including bottled water, cookies and my favorite strawberry and watermelon hard candies. It felt like an oasis. I helped myself to a handful of candy and relaxed on the couch while Dana took Brad for a ride in the Cub over Lake Powell and the surrounding canyons.

Hotel rooms were surprisingly hard to find in Page that day, and we ended up at an overpriced, mediocre, no-name motel. Brad was living in a group house with a bunch of other twenty-something guys, so staying at his place wasn't an option. But the hotel's air conditioner worked and the bathroom was clean, so we settled in for an afternoon of internet surfing and book writing.

The following morning we met Brad for breakfast before heading off on what would turn out to be the longest leg of our trip. We planned to fly from Page to Monument Valley and then on to Cortez, Colorado, a flight of a little over two hours that would include sightseeing in Monument Valley. When we arrived at the buttes, visibility was relatively good for flying, but haze kept our photos from turning out as clear as we'd hoped. After a few minutes we were ready to move on.

By this time, we had been in the air for quite a while and were getting tired. We decided we didn't want to fly to Cortez, which would mean a time and fuel-consuming climb. Bypassing Cortez also meant we would need to find a safe location to do an off-airport touch-and-go in order to tag the state of Colorado. A *touch-and-go* is when the pilot descends for a normal landing, but takes off again as soon as at least one wheel touches the ground.

This is essentially what we did on the deserted beach in Georgia during our flight to retrieve the Cub earlier that year.

Finding the Four Corners monument at the geographic confluence of New Mexico, Colorado, Utah, and Arizona was easy using our GPS. From there, we headed northeast into Colorado, but the terrain was not smooth enough to facilitate a safe touch-and-go on the dirt. We continued flying northeast for a few miles and located what turned out to be Route 160, the only road in sight. As we descended to scope out a suitable stretch of road, we noticed two cars heading toward us. Dana maintained a safe altitude until the cars were about a half mile behind us, then descended and performed a quick touch-and-go, followed by a climbing right turn to the southeast toward Farmington, New Mexico.

We laughed together about how we had managed to include Colorado without burning time and energy we didn't have to fly all the way to Cortez. This also allowed us to make it to Albuquerque for the night, putting the hostile terrain behind us for good.

Chapter 18
Going Home

The last week of our trip passed by quickly, and brought a few pleasant surprises. We departed Albuquerque on August 17 and followed Interstate 40 eastbound toward Amarillo, Texas. Even though the terrain was mostly flat and dry, we began to notice more signs of life and civilization below us with each mile we traversed: residential neighborhoods, farms, occasional stands of leafy trees, several green fields, and lots of traffic on I-40.

We followed the highway for a long time, amusing ourselves by reading roadside billboards and observing the animated ebb and flow of the vehicles below, just as we would if we were driving instead of flying. I spotted a truck with "CFI" emblazoned on its trailer in large red letters, and thought of how cool it was that Dana and I were both flight instructors, commonly referred to in the industry as CFIs.

I thought about how we've taught dozens of students to use maps and landmarks to avoid getting lost during a flight, to always know where they are without relying on navigation equipment that can break down just when they need it the most. Dana and I used our GPS extensively during our trip around the country, mostly for convenience and efficiency, but we never relied on it exclusively to determine our position. It was more relaxing and entertaining, anyway, to follow a truck on I-40 than to follow a computer generated line on the tiny screen of our portable GPS.

I thought about my first cross country flight as a student pilot, back when "cross country" meant, by FAA definition, flying to an airport at least 50 miles away from where I started. Now, I was literally flying *across the country* and back, traveling thousands of miles, in an airplane that was smaller and slower than the Cessna 152 that dutifully delivered me, and me alone, to a nearly deserted airport at the tip of the Maryland panhandle on a cool, clear afternoon in October 2002.

We landed mid-morning in Santa Rosa, New Mexico, for a short break and fuel. It was already starting to get hot. As we taxied over to the self-serve fuel pump, we noticed a Piper Cub parked there and wondered if maybe we'd crossed paths with its pilot back in Oshkosh. A man in khaki shorts and a wide-rimmed hat emerged from a nearby building, and we stopped to introduce ourselves.

"Is that your Cub?" Dana asked.

"Yes it is," the man said.

"I'm Dana Holladay," Dana replied, extending his hand with a smile.

"Bern Heimos. It's nice to meet you," the man said as he shook Dana's hand.

Dana and I instantly realized who he was. "Bern, we spoke on the phone late last year! My wife, Meredith, and I are the ones flying a Cub to all 48 lower states. We're the ones who called to ask about flying our Cub through the mountains."

Bern also realized who we were and began to laugh. He was the Cub pilot from California with whom we'd spoken by phone before we purchased our Cub, when we started planning our trip. The same guy whose name came up in our conversation with the Dyersville, Iowa airport manager a few weeks earlier. Bern hadn't flown to Oshkosh that year because he had to work. It was by pure coincidence that we met that morning at Santa

Rosa, because Bern had left California two days prior and was on his way to New York.

We hugged one another like old friends, not believing how lucky we were to be standing there together, beside our beautiful old airplanes. Bern is an accomplished pilot with hundreds of hours of cross-country flying experience. He's flown his Cub from coast to coast several times, and makes a long trip like this once a year. An avid blogger and photographer, Bern loves sharing his passion for aviation with others and is the person who confirmed that our Cub would make it over the mountains easily because he'd done it many times before, in a Cub with slightly less horsepower than ours. He posted the following on his blog a couple of days after our chance encounter:

Day 3–August 17, 2012–Gallup, NM to Guymon, Oklahoma

We have heard considerable talk about who will fly adventures across America in vintage airplanes when the current group of enthusiasts hangs up their wings. Perhaps this encounter will explain: Out of sheer coincidence or possibly serendipitously Dana and Meredith landed at Santa Rosa, New Mexico for fuel at the same time the Cub and I did. Ironically both of the Cubs toured Monument Valley the day before. Now for the twist. Dana and Meredith had seen this website last year and emailed me for some flight planning information. Eventually we talked on the phone last winter as they explained their passion to land in all 48 lower states with their Cub.

Today, when Dana introduced himself and Meredith to me and I to them, broad smiles of disbelief brightened all three of our faces. The next hour was filled with an exchange of stories so laced with the passion for flying vintage airplanes across America that by the end of the hour, all of our collective feet were at least a foot off the ground.

So back to the question who will replace my generation when the time comes to hang up our wings. The answer was crystal clear today. Dana and Meredith and many pilots of their generation embody every ounce of the passion needed to carry on what was started long before this pilot was born. Now doesn't that just make you want to smile for a few months?

We visited with Bern for close to an hour, until heat and hunger started to get the best of us, and we knew it was time to leave. We took off together and followed each other for a few miles, then lost sight of Bern as we continued east toward our lunch stop in Tucumcari, New Mexico.

I was looking forward to seeing Tucumcari because it was one of the old rest stops along historic Route 66, which opened in 1926 and served as a major east-west route from Chicago to Los Angeles for nearly six decades. Over the years, portions of the route were absorbed by the Interstate Highway System, though some sections remain as historic byways, like the section passing through downtown Tucumcari, parallel to I-40.

We hopped in the courtesy car at the Tucumcari airport and drove hungrily toward Route 66, expecting to see car loads of tourists spilling into a string of kitschy gift shops, art deco diners and drive-ins. Instead, we found many of the businesses abandoned, with boarded up windows and peeling paint. There were a few motels with the classic retro arrow-shaped neon vacancy sign protruding from the front office, looking as if the last time anyone had stayed there was during the Kennedy administration. One of the motels had a corroded Cessna 140 airplane parked in the front yard, but we couldn't for the life of us figure out why.

We drove along for a few more miles, wondering if we were going to have to forage for food at the next gas station, until we saw a Tex-Mex restaurant that was open with a half-dozen cars parked out front. Inside we found a small gift shop selling Route 66 memorabilia along with brochures for a few other businesses in town that were operated by the same woman who owns the restaurant. To our dismay, it appeared that Tucumcari had devolved into a struggling one-horse town and our visit there ended shortly after we'd downed our plate of enchiladas.

The afternoon turbulence and the enchiladas didn't agree with me as we bumped our way along toward Amarillo, where we were set to spend the evening with one of Dana's old high school friends from Richmond. Jan Hodges and her husband, who were in town visiting Jan's mother, had reserved for us the guest suite in her mother's condominium complex. Jan is an artist and gave us the nickel art tour of Amarillo including the Cadillac Ranch, The Big Texan and A Huge Pair of Legs. By the time we finished eating dinner at a barbecue restaurant near the condo, it was almost 10 p.m. and we were exhausted and ready for bed.

When we left Amarillo the following morning after Dana gave Jan and her husband rides in the Cub, our thoughts turned to Atlanta where we'd visit with my aunt, uncle and cousin, who live there. We estimated it would take us another four days to reach Georgia, because we had several more states to cover first: Oklahoma, Missouri, Arkansas, Louisiana, Mississippi and Alabama. A straight line from Amarillo to Atlanta would take us relatively close to all of those states except Louisiana, which required a substantial diversion to the south.

The Louisiana stop was the most difficult for me from a motivation perspective, because I knew the only reason we were going there was to satisfy our 48-state goal. There wasn't anything in particular there that we wanted to see. At the time, I was more motivated by my desire to get out of the turbulence and out of the airplane as soon as possible. I really needed Dana to be my cheerleader, to help me focus more on our goal and less on my nausea.

"We can't skip Louisiana, Mer," Dana said. "We have to touch down in all 48 states! It's only about 200 miles to the border. You can do it!"

And I did. The flight wasn't as long as I thought it would be, and I felt a real sense of accomplishment when we touched down at a small airstrip in Lake Providence. We parked in the grass under a shady tree and watched as an older man labored to attach a thick black hose filled with pesticides to a crop duster that landed right behind us. The young pilot of the crop duster got out of his plane with the turboprop engine still running to take a quick break, while the older man filled the sprayer tanks in the plane. Within minutes the hose was removed and the pilot was back in the plane, heavy with chemicals and lumbering down the runway for takeoff in the afternoon heat.

The older man waved goodbye to us as we followed the crop duster out, then turned east toward Yazoo City, Mississippi, our last overnight stop before Atlanta. We crossed the Mississippi River and noted that its levees were wide enough to serve as emergency landing strips for the Cub, though there were plenty of open fields all around. The air was smooth and I felt my body relax into the seat as we cruised over flat, green farmland. Cellular coverage was good in that area, so I got online and researched hotels and restaurants at our destination. I was relieved to find a Hampton Inn, one of our favorites, just a few miles from the airport. All we had to do was find a car to get there.

We landed at the Yazoo County Airport and noticed that one of the hangar doors was open. Inside was a large crop duster similar to the one we saw at our last stop. As we tied the plane down near the hangar, a young man in a pickup truck pulled up next to us to see if we needed any help. We told him we needed a car for the night, and asked if the airport had one we could borrow. While Dana unloaded our bags, the man drove me over to the courtesy car. It was nicer than we expected, and in a few minutes we were on our way to the hotel.

Dinner in Yazoo City was a bit of a disappointment, however. We managed to find what is probably the only self-proclaimed steak house in America that does not serve real butter, but instead offers those little yellow containers of artificial "buttery spread." Their prices were high and they charged extra for sharing a plate. Dana and I almost always share a meal when we go to a restaurant, because the portions are usually large enough to feed two adults, and it saves money. Still, we were thankful to be safely on the ground, in a quiet air-conditioned room, and looked forward to our flight to Atlanta the next morning.

We only had to stop for fuel once on our way to Atlanta, and chose to have lunch in Tuscaloosa, Alabama, a medium-size city that's home to the University of Alabama. We parked the Cub at Dixie Air Services, one of two FBOs at the airport. The staff highly recommended that we eat at Dreamland Bar-B-Que and put us in a nearly brand new car to get there. The chopped pork plate and banana pudding were insanely good, and made up for the previous night's lackluster steak experience. Between the delicious lunch and the anticipation of seeing my family in just a few short hours, I was feeling pretty good that afternoon.

The flight from Tuscaloosa to Atlanta was uneventful, and we enjoyed a beautiful view of the city during our approach to the Peachtree-Dekalb Airport, where Dana gave me that magical seaplane ride two years earlier. My aunt and uncle, Debbie and

Gillespie Kirkland, were waiting by the fence to greet us when we arrived. It was nice to spend a couple of days there relaxing in familiar surroundings, knowing that we were in the home stretch of our incredible journey.

We left Atlanta on August 23 and made it to Beckley, West Virginia, for what would be our last night away from home for a while. The next day we enjoyed great weather and a smooth ride across the Virginia-West Virginia border and into the Shenandoah Valley Regional Airport, where we stopped for lunch. By 4 p.m. we arrived in Frederick, Maryland for a brief visit with our friend and fellow pilot, Jill Tallman, at AOPA headquarters. Jill, who writes for *AOPA Pilot* magazine, had asked us to stop by so she and a staff videographer could interview us for a story they planned to run on the AOPA Web site a few days later. Jill followed up with an article in the November issue of the magazine that discussed our trip and cleverly leaked our good news to the world. We can't thank Jill, and the entire staff of AOPA, enough for all of their support during our incredible journey.

As we climbed into the Cub to complete the last leg of our trip, I decided on a whim that I wanted to fly, and Dana gladly offered me the controls. For the first time in weeks I felt completely relaxed as I taxied out to the runway at Frederick, took off and turned to the east toward Fallston, with the setting sun behind us and the cool evening air blowing on my face. With one hand on the control sick and the other resting on my belly, I smiled and marveled at the fact that I was pregnant, happy, and flying a beautiful airplane with the man I love. Even though the last few weeks of traveling had been a little rough on my body, my spirit was intact. Life was good.

The air was completely still and I made a smooth landing at Fallston. Our journey was complete. The airport manager had left a hand-made sign in our parking space that read, "Welcome Back to W42." We emptied the plane and tied it back in its space, right where we'd started two months before.

While we waited for my friend Alison to arrive to give us a ride home, we walked the length of the runway and noticed how tall the corn had grown while we were gone. Two months had passed by in the blink of an eye. We had seen and done so much in that short span, and it would take some time for it all to really sink in.

We didn't know it at the time, but someone was watching us walk the runway. During the last week of December 2012, as we were making final preparations to publish this book, I got an email from a man who also kept his airplane at Fallston. He wrote:

> *I'm at Fallston and landed after you got back from your flying adventure. I was going to stop after I put my Bonanza away and chat. However when I drove past your hangar your stuff was there but you were not. As I turned the corner to exit, I looked down the runway and saw you two down the runway embracing each other. I was thinking to myself at the time, what wonderful symbolism, having spent the last couple of months together in close quarters and you still want to be together. Then I saw your wedding photo you posted recently and it reminded me of that moment and what would have been a perfect end of the adventure photo. I didn't take the photo as it seemed to me to be a private moment. I just wanted to let you know that I witnessed the conclusion to what must have been a fantastic adventure. You are truly blessed to have found each other.*

Before we got in the car to leave, we gave our Cub a friendly pat on the cowling to thank it for not letting us down.

Chapter 19
The Adventure Continues

Dana and I were back to work instructing within a few days of our return. Dana had a full roster of students with Fleming Aviation, the sport pilot training center at our home airport in Gaithersburg, Maryland. I had lined up a few other students before we left on our trip, and started getting calls from regular customers once everyone realized we were back in town. It was good to be busy, and better to know that we didn't have to rely on our savings to pay the bills.

My nausea had subsided to a tolerable level and, with more moderate temperatures at home compared to what we'd experienced during our trip, I was able to fly and teach quite comfortably all day long. Dana and I really enjoy spending our days together at the airport, doing what we love to do. We often pass each other on the taxiway and wave, or hear each other's voice on the radio and say a quick hello. I still get a rush when I hear Dana talk on the radio, just like I did that warm afternoon in Atlanta when he took me up for my first ride in that little yellow seaplane.

Teaching people how to fly is such an important part of each of our lives, and we take great pride in helping our students become competent, safe and responsible pilots. Dana and I have each invested many years and thousands of dollars earning our flight instructor certificates, and it's rewarding to be able to use those skills to help others achieve their goals. Still, being a full-time flight instructor is demanding work that generally offers few financial benefits such as company sponsored health insurance, retirement plans or paid days off. You really have to hustle to get ahead, but we are self-starters and entrepreneurs who wouldn't have it any other way.

We are also frugal realists, and as such made the prudent but difficult decision to sell the Cub. Not having a loan payment each month would greatly improve our bottom line, and we knew that even if we could afford to keep it, we wouldn't get to enjoy it as much as we had during the summer because we were so busy instructing. During our week at Oshkosh we met a couple from Indiana who fell in love with our Cub, and made us an offer on the spot. After some friendly negotiations we agreed on a deal, and Dana delivered the airplane to them in September. We missed being airplane owners, but were thankful for the financial relief, especially with our baby on the way.

My first prenatal doctor's appointment was on August 28, the week after we got home. Dana had wanted to come with me to the appointment, but his day was packed with flights and we couldn't afford to turn customers away. I didn't really know what to expect at the time, so I didn't think it was a big deal that Dana wasn't there.

The doctor checked my vitals and then, to my surprise, rolled a portable sonogram (ultrasound) machine next to the exam table so she could confirm a fetus was present. I got to see the little sac with a tiny blob in it, and heard its rapid heartbeat. I cried with joy when I saw and heard our baby inside me, and immediately regretted Dana wasn't there to share that incredible moment. I never thought I'd get to experience being a mother, and yet there I was, seeing and hearing my baby—our baby—for the very first time.

The doctor sent me home with a small black and white screen shot of the sonogram image. It reminds me of one of those three-frame photo reels sold at shopping mall kiosks, where couples or best friends go to take spontaneous photos of themselves goofing off. That first sonogram image was concrete evidence that Dana and I were going to be parents. According to the doctor's measurements of the size of the fetus, I was about eight weeks along in the pregnancy, which meant the baby was conceived during the first few days of our trip, while we were in New York (just like the first time) and would be born within a week of my 41st birthday.

A few weeks later, I returned for another doctor's appointment and this time Dana came with me. It was comforting to hold his hand while we listened to the baby's heartbeat. By that time I had already developed a subtle baby bump, and with each passing week it became more obvious as my belly blossomed.

On November 5 we returned for my 18-week sonogram. This was a more detailed scan where they evaluated the baby's anatomy and attempted to determine the baby's gender. The technician who performed the sonogram had a concerned, concentrated look on her face while she was working, which I found a bit disconcerting. I was expecting this to be a fun appointment but from the start it felt a bit stressful. We asked the technician if she was able to tell whether it was a boy or a girl, and she said she was pretty sure it was a girl. Dana was able to see the monitor but it was facing away from me so I couldn't see it. He was smiling, though, watching our little baby's arms and feet flop around. She was alive. She was real.

After about half an hour of rubbing my belly with warm blue jelly and the imaging wand, the technician said she wanted to get a second opinion on something. The second technician scanned me for a few minutes and then decided to ask for another opinion, calling in the chief radiologist. While we waited for him to arrive, they asked me walk around the room to try to get the baby to move so that they could get a better view of her.

The radiologist came in and took the controls. He was concerned that the baby's stomach appeared higher than it's supposed to be, but said the image wasn't entirely clear due to the baby's position, and I'd probably need another scan. He didn't seem terribly concerned, though, so Dana and I left the office feeling positive. They told us that my doctor would call to discuss the results of the sonogram once she got the full report from the radiologist in a few days.

That was around 11 a.m. on Monday. Later that afternoon, I had a voice mail message from the doctor's office saying that I should expect a call from the doctor at 4 p.m. on Wednesday to discuss the results. But at 8 a.m. on Tuesday I got another message, this one from my doctor personally, saying that I should call her right away. I was flying when the call came in, and by the time I landed and finished debriefing with my student in the pilot's lounge, she was calling again. I answered the phone and within a few seconds nearly dropped it to the floor.

"Meredith, based on yesterday's ultrasound we suspect that your baby has a condition called congenital diaphragmatic hernia," she said. "This is very serious and could be life threatening for the baby. There is a hole in the baby's diaphragm and her stomach has traveled up through the hole into her chest. I've scheduled an appointment with you for this afternoon at our high-risk obstetrics facility in Gaithersburg for a second ultrasound to confirm the diagnosis. You should bring your husband and take lots of notes."

I was sitting down but my legs began to quiver. Did she just say what I think she said?

"Meredith, do you have any questions?"

I didn't really know what to ask. I was stunned. But I forced myself not to panic, to focus on the facts, on the immediate areas of concern.

"Doctor, is there any risk of me having another miscarriage? Is there anything that I could be doing in my daily activities that inadvertently could make the situation worse?"

I thought about our trip in the Cub, the smoke, the fuel, the turbulence, the heat. I thought about whether this news meant I'd have to stop flying and teaching for the remainder of the pregnancy.

"No, there is nothing you could have done to cause this, and nothing you are doing right now has any effect on the situation," she said. I was relieved, but still needed more information. "Neither you nor the baby is in any immediate danger. As long as the baby is in the womb, her needs are being met. But the baby could have serious problems after birth when it's time for her to breathe on her own, because her stomach is occupying the space where her lungs should be growing. We won't know for certain what to expect until we do more tests."

With that, I thanked her, wrote down the address of the office where we needed to go later that day, and hung up the phone. Dana was in the other room with his student. I went in and told him I needed to see him as soon as he was finished. He could tell from the look on my face that something was wrong. A few minutes later he came in and I unloaded the news. We both sat down on the sofa. I started crying.

"What is happening? Why is this happening?" Neither of us knew the answer. We just lay there for a few minutes holding each other, letting the emotional wave run through us.

"Come on, let's go home," Dana said quietly, holding my hand and helping me up off of the sofa. We called our students and canceled our lessons for the rest of the day.

As soon as we got home I went online and searched for information about congenital diaphragmatic hernia, or CDH. At first glance none of it was too encouraging. Babies born with CDH need surgery shortly after birth to repair the misalignment of internal organs and patch the hole in the diaphragm. Even if the surgery is successful, CDH babies require weeks, months or even years of extensive medical care and therapy to recover from the surgery and cope with other complications that can arise, like pulmonary and digestive system problems. The main problem CDH babies have immediately after birth is trouble breathing, because the extra organs in the chest compress the lungs and prevent them from growing during the pregnancy. The size of the lungs at birth seemed to be a key factor in the likelihood of survival. CDH babies also sometimes have trouble eating normally and may require a temporary feeding tube to sustain them during the recovery period.

We drove to the doctor's office in silence, both of us stunned at what was happening. After a long wait we finally got into the exam room. A technician performed the ultrasound and this time, I could watch the entire thing on the monitor, as could Dana. She was much more upbeat than the previous technician, but nonetheless confirmed that the baby's stomach was inside her chest, pushing her heart to one side and compressing one of her lungs, which was not visible on the scan. All else seemed relatively normal. The doctor came in and agreed with the technician's findings. He was young and very blunt in his delivery, but we appreciated his no-nonsense approach, because as pilots, that's how we tend to deal with things as well. Just the facts.

The doctor urged me to have an amniocentesis on the spot to rule out any genetic defects that could also be present. In September, when I had the first ultrasound to confirm the pregnancy, that doctor had offered me an amniocentesis as an optional procedure to check for genetic defects, but I declined because of the risk of miscarriage from the procedure—anywhere from about one in 500 to one in 200, according to various reputable sources I'd found online. Besides, every other test I'd had up to that point indicated that I was healthy, and neither Dana nor I had any family history of genetic defects, which if we did, would increase the odds that our baby could be born with one. I worried about doing something invasive and unnecessary that could cause another miscarriage. I didn't want to have to go through that again, and worse, have it be my fault.

But now we had a real, immediate problem to deal with—the CDH diagnosis—and faced the possibility that the baby could have even more serious problems lurking in its genes, something deadly that we had not considered, something that would make her already complicated situation even worse. There is no known genetic or environmental cause for CDH, but all things considered the amnio seemed like a no brainer at that point, so I signed the consent form while the doctor prepared the very large needle to insert into my belly.

I am terrified of needles but just kept telling myself, "Relax. You are doing this for her. This is for her." I couldn't stop shaking and was afraid I would knock the needle out of position and botch the test, but the doctor assured me it would be all right. The amnio was very uncomfortable and I trembled the entire time, but it was soon over.

The doctor told us he'd have preliminary results from the lab within 72 hours, and the first cut would check for the most serious chromosomal defects that would in all likelihood mean certain death for the child. He wanted us to be prepared to make the difficult decision to terminate the pregnancy if the tests revealed the baby had little or no hope of survival. Fortunately we didn't have to make that decision, because two days later we learned the initial results came back negative, meaning no chromosomal defects were detected. The remainder of the results were also normal.

Meanwhile, the doctor suggested we schedule an appointment with a team of specialists at Children's National Medical Center in Washington, D.C. He said other than the stress of dealing with the diagnosis, my pregnancy should progress normally and last the full term, but they would induce labor on a specific date during my 39th week when the entire surgical team would be waiting at Children's to care for our sick newborn the moment she arrived. I would deliver the baby at Washington Hospital Center, which is right next door to Children's.

A few days later I spoke with our patient representative at Children's, who would be coordinating all of our baby's care. She scheduled us for an all-day visit at the hospital on November 13, which would include several tests followed by a meeting with members of the pediatric surgical team. From what we'd read online, it takes a large group of specialists and lots of equipment to care for a CDH baby. Our journey to parenthood was shaping up to be another interesting adventure.

We arrived at Children's a little before 6 a.m. on November 13 and went immediately to the radiology department, where I was scheduled for an MRI and several detailed ultrasounds to better determine the extent of our baby's condition. The tests took a very long time to complete, but were not at all painful or uncomfortable. The worst part was waiting patiently through them all so we could get to the meeting with the team to discuss the results.

By about 2 p.m. the tests were complete and we were escorted to a small office where we met with the head nurse and one of the surgeons. The surgeon told us the day's tests showed our baby's stomach, as well as portions of her small intestine and liver, were inside her chest and pressing against her lungs and heart. The good news from the cardiologist was that her heart was structurally normal and, despite being out of place, was functioning just fine. We also learned her right lung, while a bit squished, appeared to be of normal size and the left lung would grow after the surgery made room for it to expand. This positive news meant we had fewer things to worry about in a growing list of potential complications.

"So," Dana said, "what are her chances of living a normal, healthy life?" We like to get right to the point. The surgeon, anticipating this loaded but important question because he's heard it from hundreds of parents like us over the last three decades, answered calmly and confidently.

"Our first CDH patient is now 28 years old and in medical school," he said with a guarded smile. "So it is possible for these kids to live happy, healthy and productive lives. But there are no guarantees. Some CDH babies who appear to have a good chance of survival don't make it. Others who are given slim odds defy them. There's just no clear way to know what to expect. It all depends on how stable the baby is after birth, and how well she responds to treatment. But given that your baby has no apparent genetic abnormalities, has no apparent cardiac defects, and has substantial lung growth on one side, I am reasonably optimistic that she will do well."

That's all we needed to hear.

As we close this final chapter in our book, a new chapter in our lives is about to unfold. I began this book by stating that I hoped that my darkest days were behind me, and now more than ever I believe that's true. Because no matter what happens during the rest of my pregnancy, no matter what the outcome of this birth, I have peace knowing that Dana and I are in this together, that we have each other, and that our love can sustain and overcome any challenges that we may face in life, no matter how daunting.

We chose to name our daughter Alexandra, after the late Alexandra Tolstoy, daughter of the late author Leo Tolstoy. Alexandra Tolstoy was a strong, well educated Russian woman who fought to defend the civil rights and freedoms of people suffering from oppression in Eastern Europe during the mid 1900s. One of those people was my grandmother, Valentina Tcherniavsky, who was the only one of 13 children in her family to survive an attack by the Stalin regime on their rural farming village in southern Ukraine. She and her husband, Andrej, married in 1942 and hitchhiked more than 1,000 miles to safety in what was then the British occupied sector of Germany following World War II. It was there that Valentina, in 1946 at the age of 41, gave birth to my father. Andrej died of complications following surgery for a stomach ulcer while my father was still an infant. ("Surgery was a dicey proposition in rural postwar Europe," Dad noted.) Granny and Dad made it to the United States in 1951 through the auspices of the Tolstoy Foundation, a humanitarian relief organization founded by Alexandra Tolstoy. Were it not for her efforts, I might not be here today to share this story.

Our greatest hope is that our little Alexandra will survive her birth and surgery, that she will recover quickly, and thrive. I dream of taking her up for her first flight a few years from now, just us two girls in an airplane together, enjoying the sky. I dream of Dana carrying her on his shoulders high above the crowd during the air show in Oshkosh, and of the two of us walking her up to Compass Hill. I dream about Dana and I fighting over who will get to endorse Alex for her first solo flight. I dream of the three of us playing on the beach together, and of Dana walking her down the aisle at her wedding when we are old and gray.

We hope that Alex will inherit our strength and will to live, because she's going to need it to get through the extraordinary challenges that await her during her first moments on earth. We don't pray for miracles or engage in other forms of wishful thinking. We deal with the facts, with the science, and rely on our experience and our love to guide us through. Still, we are human and we hope for a positive outcome. Because being happy and staying positive feels a lot better than being sad, better than worrying needlessly about things that we cannot control.

So if you are listening down there in my belly, little Alexandra, your mommy has just one favor to ask of you: *"Fly the airplane. Don't worry about anything else. Just fly."*

Afterword

Thank you for reading this book. To follow the continuing story of our journey to parenthood and our life as pilots, and to view additional photos from our trip, please visit our Web site, www.holladayaviation.com.

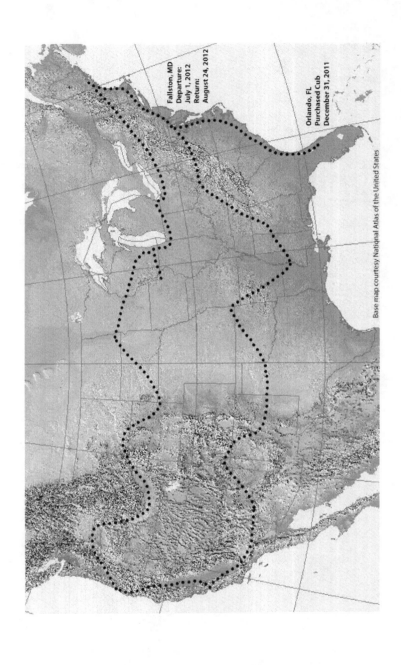

Fallston, MD
Departure:
July 1, 2012
Return:
August 24, 2012

Orlando, FL
Purchased Cub
December 31, 2011

Base map courtesy National Atlas of the United States

12/31/11—Fernandina Beach, FL; Touch-and-go on a deserted beach in Georgia; Beaufort, SC

1/1/12—Ocean Isle Beach, SC; Washington, NC; Kill Devil Hills, NC; Norfolk, VA

1/2/12—Leonardtown, MD; Fallston, MD

7/1/12—Middletown, DE; Lumberton, NJ; White Plains, NY

7/5/12—Meriden, CT; Pawtucket, RI; Lawrence, MA

7/6/12—Brunswick, ME; Bar Harbor, ME

7/8/12—Lewiston, ME; Bristol, NH; Springfield, VT

7/10/12—Johnstown, NY; Cortland, NY

7/11/12—Olean, NY; Greenville, PA; Wadsworth, OH

7/12/12—Lagrange, OH; Wakeman, OH; Put In Bay, OH; Sturgis, MI; Michigan City, IN; Wilmot, WI

7/19/12—Monroe, WI; Galena, IL; Dyersville, IA

7/21/12—Hartford, WI

7/22/12—Oshkosh, WI

7/27/12—Marshfield, WI; Eau Claire, WI

7/28/12—Cambridge, MN; Alexandria, MN; Wahpeton, ND; Aberdeen, SD

7/29/12—Pierre, SD; Valentine, NE; Rapid City, SD; Sturgis, SD

7/30/12—Spearfish, SD; Gillette, WY; Sheridan, WY; Columbus, MT

7/31/12—Townsend, MT; Canyon Ferry, MT

8/1/12—West Yellowstone, MT

8/3/12—Blackfoot, ID; Burley, ID; Mountain Home, ID; Nampa, ID

8/6/12—Baker City, OR; Hermiston, OR; Yakima, WA; Hood River, OR

8/9/12—McMinville, OR; Florence, OR; Medford, OR

8/10/12—Weed, CA; Red Bluff, CA; Sonoma, CA

8/11/12—Hollister, CA

8/12/12—Corcoran, CA; Bakersfield, CA; Tehachapi, CA; Lancaster, CA

8/14/12—Daggett, CA; Boulder City, NV

8/15/12—St. George, UT; Page, AZ

8/16/12—Off-airport touch-and-go near the Four Corners Monument in Colorado; Farmington, NM; Albuquerque, NM

8/17/12—Santa Rosa, NM; Tucumcari, NM; Amarillo, TX

8/18/12—Canadian, TX; Fairview, OK; Ponca City, OK

8/19/12—Neosho, MO; Springdale, AR

8/20/12—Hot Springs, AR; Warren, AR; Lake Providence, LA; Yazoo City, MS

8/21/12—Tuscaloosa, AL; Atlanta, GA

8/23/12—Copperhill, TN; Harlan, KY; Beckley, WV

8/24/12—Hot Springs, VA; Shenandoah, VA; Frederick, MD; Fallston, MD

Made in the USA
Charleston, SC
22 February 2013